Words of Praise for
Get More Done in Less Time!

If I drew up a list of people I know who are tops at helping you get organized and on track, Donna Otto's name would be right with the best. Donna has been a good friend for years, and I know she has a rock-solid commitment to Christ, her family, and to helping others gain control of their "hectic" lives and schedules. IF YOU'RE READY TO GET BACK TO DOING THE IMPORTANT THINGS— INSTEAD OF SEEING ALL YOUR TIME SWALLOWED UP BY THE URGENT—THEN GET *GET MORE DONE IN LESS TIME!*

—*John Trent, Ph.D.*
President, Encouraging Words

GET MORE DONE IN LESS TIME! WILL GIVE HOPE TO WOMEN WHO DESIRE ORDER IN THEIR LIVES—lives often lived in fragmented, high-stress situations. Donna puts new meaning to the idea that there TRULY is a "time for every purpose under heaven"—and she does it with flair.

—*Daisy Hepburn*
Heritage Ministries

DONNA OTTO IS ONE OF THE MOST INNOVATIVE PEOPLE I KNOW. Hers is the epitome of a well-balanced life: She has learned to prioritize her time—putting the Lord first, followed by family, friends, and career. Donna is creative, energetic, and a self-disciplinarian. It all comes together to help you and me in the most uncomplicated, easy-to-understand *Get More Done in Less Time!*

—*Donna Wild Foss*
Author of *A Proud American*

GET MORE DONE IN LESS TIME

DONNA OTTO

HARVEST HOUSE PUBLISHERS
Eugene, Oregon 97402

GET MORE DONE IN LESS TIME

Copyright © 1995 by Donna Otto
Published by Harvest House Publishers
Eugene, Oregon 97402

Library of Congress Cataloging-in-Publication Data

Otto, Donna.
    Get more done in less time—and get on with the fun stuff! / Donna
Otto.
      p.   cm.
    ISBN 1-56507-253-7
    1. Women—United States—Time management. I. Title.
HQ1221.0693   1994
640'.43'082—dc20   94-29541
                                                  CIP

Printed in the United States of America.

95 96 97 98 99 00 01 02 — 10 9 8 7 6 5 4 3 2

Contents

With deep devotion I dedicate this book
to the two most valuable people in my life . . .
my steadfast husband David and
my joyful daughter Anissa.

Acknowledgments

My thanks to the following people:

Mike Hyatt, Robert Wolgemuth, Steve Scott, and Janet Thoma. Each of you made the first edition of this book possible.

Rick Johnson, the computer man. I am getting it!

Diane Ortega, of Carstens, for "the look."

Betty Fletcher, an understanding editor. Can we go sailing now?

Eileen Mason. You truly do see the BIG PICTURE. Thank you so much.

Get More Done
in Less Time

When I first met Donna Otto I knew we were kindred spirits
Our organizational hearts just seemed to bond together, as well
as our "fun stuff"!

To be in her home is like spending time in the comfort of a
charming, warm, loving bed and breakfast You can feel her love
for the Lord in all her organization skills. She moves freely,
finding whatever is needed. It is as though I cannot see her
working at her home and yet everything seems to get done in less
time and with less effort. This creates time to enjoy each other's
fellowship and do the things that give our friendship the pleasure
of our kindred spirits.

You will so enjoy this book and be thrilled when your family
sees the results of how little time her plan takes. They will enjoy
seeing mom once again—and enjoy the "fun stuff" in life as a
family and with friends.

Donna has a heart for happy women, happy homes, happy
children, and happy husbands.

Let her writing enter into your life and home. You will be so
excited, you'll want to try all of her ideas for creating more time.

Thank you, God, for Donna Otto, my speaking colleague and
friend.

—Emilie Barnes
Author of *More Hours in My Day*
and *The Spirit of Loveliness*

1

The Common Start, the Uncommon Finish

T *here was a problem worrying the female popula-*
tion of Phoenix, Arizona. I mean, there had to
be. I was asked to teach a three-evening workshop at a local
college on "Home Management for Housewives." I had
been assigned a seminar room capable of holding 15 people
comfortably, but more than 275 women showed up to attend
the first session. The college officials were overwhelmed.
They transferred us to the campus auditorium. As we
walked to the auditorium, I studied the faces of the women
in the crowd.

You might have been among them; if not literally, then
in kind. They ranged in age from 17 to 81. Some were well-
dressed; others were making do. A few were smiling, but
most were tired and weary looking. They had problems.

"...and she's supposed to be good," I overheard one
woman say. "She'll have to be to keep me awake after the
day I put in. All three of my boys had ball games scheduled
for..."

I lost the rest of the conversation as we entered the
auditorium. Mrs. Graham, the campus director for evening
studies, met me at the door.

"Oh, Mrs. Otto," she said. "I...I had no idea there

would be so many. I'm so terribly sorry." Her hands were actually trembling.

I smiled. "They'll probably give you a raise, Mrs. Graham. This is a wonderful turnout. Really."

She began to twist a handkerchief in her hands. "Well, I . . . I never meant it to get so out of hand. It's just that when the Women's Club canceled its monthly meeting tonight so that its members could come here and . . ."

"It's okay, it's okay," I cut in. "No problem. You can do me one favor though. Here are the keys to my car. Please have someone open my trunk and bring two full boxes of handout material here."

Mrs. Graham's mouth fell open. "You mean to say that you came with enough handouts for everyone? *Everyone?*"

"This isn't the only seminar I'm scheduled for this week," I laughed. "My trunk is filled. We're going to be just fine tonight."

"Yes, yes, I can see that now," said Mrs. Graham, a calm finally coming into her voice. "Thank goodness you practice what you preach. If I had been prepared the way you always are, this wouldn't have . . ."

I patted her shoulder. "Just get the handouts, Mrs. Graham. Things will be fine. I'll get started."

As I made my way to the podium, I again caught snatches of conversations:

". . . just help me control my laundry, I'll be happy . . ."

". . . so Tom hasn't had work for six months, and I'm on third shift . . ."

". . . could just make two of myself, then I'd be able to . . ."

". . . said she was from Chicago and recently moved out here and this is her first class in Phoenix . . ."

I stood before the large gathering and waited for the room to get perfectly quiet. I held back a few seconds in order to rivet everyone's attention on me. Then I began.

"My name is Donna Otto, and I've lived where you live." I paused, then added, "Now, I want you to be able to live where I live."

The room remained silent.

"I came from a broken home. That was a life I didn't want for myself, or my children, so I vowed to try to be the best wife possible. I've kept that vow."

I waited a moment, then continued.

"I was a single career woman who paid her own way by working at a boutique, directing a private school, selling real estate, and managing properties. The only real college training I ever received was the lessons I gained from the School of Hard Knocks. But I learned well. Today, I am a lecturer and consultant in life management.

"I've lived where you live. I know the burdens, the problems, and the heartaches of living there.

"But I've moved away from that. I'll never move back. And tonight, I want to begin showing you how I made that move.

"Then you can move, too. Here, now, is my story. . . ."

My parents married very young, and I was the first-born. My mother's family was from Persia. Mother was cool, protective, and a taskmaster. My father was Italian—passionate, energetic, and very protective—especially of his daughter, whom he considered beautiful despite a nose that did justice to my Persian-Italian heritage. Once when a teenage boy said I looked like a cross between Pinocchio and Jimmy Durante, my father, who happened to overhear the taunt, asked, "Are your hospitalization benefits current?" That ended further teasing!

My dad restored my self-esteem during those moments, but he was too strict and kept me at arm's length from the warmth I really needed. After a stormy marriage, my parents divorced when I was 12.

My mother, my brother, and I moved from our large frame house to a one-bedroom apartment and started over from scratch. Mother went to work fulltime in a candy factory, and I was left with a list of household chores and rules of housekeeping. (A daily job, for example, was to wash the top of the refrigerator.) I had to clean and cook by myself on weekdays and assist my mother's vigorous attacks on the tough dirt on weekends. I was taught responsibility and duty under my mother's reinterpretation of the old cliché "Cleanliness is next to godliness," which was "Godliness is next to cleanliness."

A tough taskmaster can make a terrific teacher. Even though I didn't enjoy the discipline, boy, did I learn!

As a married woman and mother, I have discovered that organization, love, and hospitality are the time-tested attributes that husbands and children respect most about wives and mothers. Many women have no understanding, however, of how to lead an organized life. After all, we learn good or bad habits from our moms. We don't take Home Organization 101 in college. What I learned from a mother who by necessity *and* choice was organized has led me into a career as a teacher and advisor on life management for women.

Husbands have called me and made comments like: "For eight years I've said to my wife, 'You should get up early enough to have breakfast ready. You should set the table the night before. You should schedule daily activities.' She ignored everything I said. Then you spent three hours with her, and she's begun to do all these things. I don't know why, and really, I don't *care* why. I'm just grateful."

I've had women say, "After your classes, I wanted to organize my love, as you suggested, before I organized my home. But I listened to your word of caution: 'Home organization must come first.' I got my house in order.

"My husband says that this is the most genuine act of love I could have ever shown him. Learning to be organized is not an act of selfishness, it's a discipline of love."

EARLY INFLUENCES

At every stage of my life, my father honestly believed I was Miss America. Not me. I felt ugly sometimes. I was too skinny, too tall, and had hair that was too thick and too bushy. I was the brunt of every nose joke ever created, like "Are you growing another arm in the middle of your face, Donna?"

But, as usually happens as we are growing up, we find one area of life that distinguishes us from everyone else. It may be our appearance, our athletic skills, our musical skills, our leadership skills, or some other talent that earns us a pat on the back from friends, teachers, relatives, or bosses. The awkward, skinny Donna Centanne found that her status symbol came from being "Miss Organized."

When I started high school, I bought a small spiral notebook, to which I attached tabs. I had a little section in one of my desk drawers that had files, also with tabs, to keep my papers organized. At first my classmates teased me about being so organized about everything.

"What else do you put in there besides your homework assignments?" the kids would ask as they pointed to the black notebook. "You don't have that great a social life. What are you doing?"

Some hotshot would then quip, "You training to be a spy or something?" And another would add, "What a bookworm!"

Their voices changed, however, when it came time to elect class officers or club leaders. "Let's make Donna treasurer," someone would shout. "She'll keep track of our money."

Whenever there was a party or social, a school fund-raiser or a special Christmas dance, I was asked to help organize it.

I didn't think about long-range planning until I went to work parttime in my father's real estate office during my midteen years. My father based his activities on a seven-day planner: a binder with legal-size paper, each sheet being divided into seven days. Across the top of the page, Dad wrote his appointments and the jobs he needed to do that week. He gave me one of those books right away.

Teenagers always have trouble taking orders from their parents, and I was no exception. I resisted using Dad's planner. After all, I had my little steno pad, and I always kept the appointments I made. My father was trying to stretch me, however, and eventually he won me over.

Learning basic organizational skills helped me in the job market too. One summer during a lull in my father's business, I took a parttime job in a clothing boutique as a salesclerk. Mrs. Rubel, the owner, let me use part of her desk as a place to tally my orders. Within a week on the job, I had the desk cleaned and organized. Mrs. Rubel was so impressed by my initiative, she assigned me to work the cash register and help keep the account records. I logged extra hours and drew extra pay because I evidenced good organization.

DEVELOPING A PLANNER

Later I went to work for my father as a licensed real estate agent. I was still using a notebook planner augmented by my father's long-range planning sheets, but I found it too limited for my new needs as a working adult. So I experimented with a variety of 3-ring, 6-ring, even 12-ring notebooks, which I customized with divider tabs, notecards, and folders. They were good—even functional—but never exactly right for all my needs.

Finally I saw an ad for a three-ring binder just for real estate agents. Each day page was marked so you could record appointments and expenses. Another section had forms to record properties listed and sold, interviews made, and contacts with bankers. Amortization and commission schedules were in the front of the book. The book was two or three inches deep, which was much too bulky, but I used it faithfully.

I ran into trouble, however, when I used my real estate planning book to record personal things—shopping lists, friends' telephone numbers, and my household budget. The book was not designed for that, and so it became a maze of scribbles, color codes, and dog-eared pages.

I searched bookstores, stationery outlets, and gift shops in a diligent effort to find a planner that could fit both my personal and business needs. There was no such planner. So, necessity proved once again to be the mother of invention. I went back to buying notebooks and creating my own customized planners. I modified them as each month passed. I began to get closer and closer to my dream planner.

ACCEPTING THE CHALLENGE OF CHANGE

After I married David Otto, I continued to sell real estate. As part of my ongoing training, I took classes in time management, salesmanship, and business organization and continued to modify my planner, which I have always called my daybook, to fit new needs.

A career opportunity opened up for David in Arizona, so we moved there. Now I had the opportunity to apply everything I had learned about life management to my housekeeping. I created an efficient kitchen, a labeled and organized pantry, an entertainment schedule for guests, a chores list for my daughter, and a variety of other helpful and useful procedures. I had previously shared organizational tips and aids with one or two friends and a couple of women's groups. Now more and more women's groups began to call on me to speak at their meetings. Soon I began to teach "More Hours in My Day" classes on home and family organization with a new friend, Emilie Barnes, who is the originator of this seminar.

My planner had become so essential to me, I decided to manufacture my daybook and market it under the trade name of *Donna's DATES and DOs.* Once I discovered the overwhelming costs involved in such a production effort, I gave up. I knew there was a crying need for such a product, but it was just not within my means to manufacture, publicize, distribute, market, and sell it.

During this time, David reminded me of his favorite saying: *"The common start, but the uncommon finish.* Keep your planner. Wait for an opportunity. Be ready."

Well, I did keep the planner and I did wait—for years. When I made "Accept the Challenge of Change" my goal statement for the year 1985, I didn't know why. The line just came to me one day as I was thinking about my future goals, as I do once every year. This challenge of change exceeded all my expectations, for not long after I received an invitation to write a book that would help women learn to organize their lives.

I struggled with that offer for some time because I had never written a book and doing so would require a lot of adjustments in my life. I must confess, even though I had chosen "Accept the Challenge of Change" as that year's goal, I still hated to change.

For years my family has called me a "stick in the mud." I am a woman who uses a fountain pen and carries bottles of ink with her. Oh, I know. I can get the cartridges. But the cartridge ink is not quite as nice or as rich in color as the bottled ink. So I use bottled ink. I am also a woman who still starches her husband's shirts by dipping them in boiling water and letting them dry until they become like boards. Why, I don't even like to move the furniture in my house. No, like most people, I don't like to change.

Nevertheless, I've learned that we must seek change for ourselves. We must adapt, advance, and progress. Donna Otto must *expect* to be different a year from now, just as you must expect that of yourself. And so I wrote the book. I accepted the challenge of change.

THE REAL THING

You have encountered many deceptive things in your life. There never was a real Betty Crocker or a real Miss Lonelyhearts or a real Aunt Jemima or a real Uncle Sam. They were all manufactured to create a human element of credibility for a marketable product. But, folks, there is a *real* Donna Otto.

I have spent time in this opening chapter introducing myself to you because I want you to know that the plans and systems and ideas in the following chapters were devised by a *real* woman. I'm someone just like you. I too have a household to run, a husband to love, a child to care for, and a speaking and writing career to manage. I too have dishwater hands (if I'm not careful) and some gray hairs, and I too must fight the battle of the bulge.

When I've failed, I've learned from it. When I've succeeded, I've capitalized on it. I've taken the seeds of organization given to me by my mother, my father, my real estate courses, my friend and colleague Emilie Barnes, and the thousands of students in my classes and seminars, and I've added my Aunt Pat's love of hospitality (you'll meet Aunt Pat in the next chapter). I've planted and nurtured the best of these ideas until they "grew" into this book.

And so I put it to you now: If you too are willing to accept the challenge of change, then read on.

Remember, "The common start, but the uncommon finish."

2

Master Time and Make the Most of It

*M*y friend Karen has three children, the youngest of whom is two-year-old Natasha. *Recently, little* Tasha had a nasty cold, which made her eyes red and her nose runny. She was miserable. While grocery shopping, her mother noticed an orange-juice machine, squeezing fresh oranges at full speed. *That's what Tasha needs*, she thought.

Back at home she poured the juice into the baby's tippee cup, put the top on, gathered Tasha in her arms, and handed her the cup. Tasha's eyes lit up as she began to drink. Karen was happy. Then, after just a few swallows, the little girl began to cry as if her heart would break. She refused to drink any more. Karen kept giving her the cup, coaxing her to drink it because she needed the vitamins. The more she tried, the more intensely Tasha resisted.

Karen was puzzled. Tasha had always loved orange juice. Perhaps it was spoiled. Karen took off the top and sipped it. *Tastes great!* she thought. But when she tried to give the cup back to Tasha, she wouldn't even take it. Throughout the day, the baby drank water, apple juice, and a little ginger ale, but never the orange juice. At day's end, Karen, in frustration, took the cup to the sink, threw out the juice, and began to wash the lid. The three tiny holes in the lid of the cup were clogged with orange pulp! No wonder the baby became so frustrated.

Karen felt like an idiot. *Three kids and I never thought to check the nozzle!* she chided herself. She is a thoughtful and loving mother, but she had not taken the time to analyze Tasha's problem carefully enough.

Before you can be organized, you need to take the time to learn the skills of organization. Throughout this book, we will be talking about the "how-tos," the "whys," and the "advantages." You may decide to use every suggestion, incorporating each one into your life. That will make you more *efficient*. You will only become more *effective*, however, if you dispense your efficiency with kindness and goodness. Love is like vitamin C. It makes people feel better, it heals their wounds, it gives them strength.

My Aunt Pat taught me how to season my mother's efficient methods with love, which is the main ingredient of a rich life. Aunt Pat knew when to let a few crumbs go unnoticed, and she valued the spontaneity of friends who knew they were always welcome. Her house always smelled of fresh bread or her special pound cake. She knew all about giggles and belly laughs. I spent every minute I could in her house. Now, food and fun in the Aunt Pat tradition are a regular part of life at the Otto house.

I knew there are special people, mentors like my Aunt Pat, in your life as well. You know who they are. You will never forget them—or their influence. And you may be such a special person to someone else. Perhaps a son or daughter or a niece or nephew. Perhaps a neighbor. What a responsibility, but what an opportunity! The purpose of this book and its concept of organization is to help you become more efficient so that you have the time to become a truly joyful person who is a blessing to others.

COMMON DENOMINATORS

You may be thinking, *How can Donna Otto tell me how to organize my life? She doesn't know me. She doesn't know my circumstances.*

Well, that's true. I don't know you. But as women, we all have certain responsibilities and identities in common. My situation is not all that different from yours.

In my classes I always ask, "How many here are women?" Everyone raises a hand.

"How many are managers of a household?"

A few hands begin to go down, until I remind the ladies, "All women are managers of a household, whether we live alone, room with another person, or keep house for our husbands and children."

Now every hand is raised.

"See, you're not so different from me after all," I say. "All women share two common denominators."

Then I ask, "How many here are wives?"

Most of the women in the room raise their hands.

"How many are mothers?"

A few hands go down, but many remain up.

Finally I ask, "How many work outside the home? Full-time? How many work parttime? How many do volunteer work?" By now most of the hands are back up in the air.

Then I say, "Many women share these additional denominators. We can think of these five common denominators as hats. We all wear the first two hats, as females and managers of some kind of household most of our lives." I place one huge wide-brimmed, black and white hat on my head, then add a smaller cleaning hat on top of the first hat (Illustration 1).

"Some of us may wear one or more of the next three hats: wives, mothers, employees." You guessed it, I pile two more hats on top of the first two. "These hats vary. At times in our lives, we wear some hats less than others (our children grow up so our role as mother diminishes), and we put another hat on (we go to work)." Off comes the tiny hat on top with the veil, and on goes the hard hat. All the ladies are laughing, but they're also listening. "Sometimes our job may be a position we held before we were married, so we put on a hat we had taken off years ago. Our lives constantly change, so we must be continually preparing for the future. Wearing these hats one at a time would be great. 'Don't cry now, honey,' you might say to your child, 'I'm being a wife.' Or you might respond to your husband's call to the office, 'I'm sorry, dear, but I'm an employee now, not a wife.'"

Illustration 1

As the laughter ebbs, I take off all the hats.

"I *can* help you organize your lives, ladies, in the areas we share in common. That's what life management is all about. But don't ever fear. I understand that we are all alike, yet different. The way we approach these five common denominators is what makes us individuals. In this class we'll also talk about the individual things each of us can do to preserve our individuality.

"The food you like to eat and cook is very different from that of your neighbors. You are an individual.

"The clothes you wear and the house and car you buy are different from your neighbors'. You are an individual.

"Although as women we face many of the same daily situations—shopping, traveling, exercising, working—no two of us behave identically. And that's great. I'd hate to think that the world was filled with Donna Ottos, all driving too fast, waving their arms as they speak, and teaching classes on organization or leading retreats. It if were, there would be a lot of things left undone in this world."

You have your own set of strengths and weaknesses. Your own supply of talent, intelligence, and creativity. Allow your creativity to grow. Knit a sweater. Weave a rug. Stitch a quilt. Enroll in a computer class. Of all things, don't allow your best friends' interests to affect your individuality. Not one of us is a mistake. We are here for a purpose. . . .

In order to fulfill your personal needs, enhance your life, and reduce your frustration, we are going to begin with some key elements of life management, which will serve to start you thinking about ways your life can be enhanced even now.

ORGANIZATION

We all have a basic need to be orderly. Every woman— those who are involved primarily in their homes as wives, mothers, and fulltime household managers and those who work outside the home—will be able to benefit from bringing her life under control. The woman herself will be the one who will reap the rewards of being organized. She will feel better, have more energy, reach goals, and be relieved of many of the pressures she has always had to cope with. She will discover a freedom she has never had before: the freedom to use her mental energies to be creative and to have fun.

No woman puts forth a great deal of effort for something unless she has the proper motivation. Organization helps you complete the tasks you start, to seize opportunities instead of missing or not recognizing them. It writes ACHIEVED across your goal page, FINISHED across your project page, WELL DONE across your checked-off to-do list! I want you automatically to plan for accomplishments in all that you undertake.

Being organized is a discipline, but it can also be fun. For instance, I hate exercise. But I've found that exercise is more tolerable—and even fun!—if my water aerobics class is fun. I begin to enjoy the leg kicks if the music suits my taste (a John Philip Sousa march, rather than jazz). If there is camaraderie among my fellow classmates—if we all come regularly and begin to tease each other about our weight problems, "Hey, Sue, did you have too much pizza over the weekend?"—then I don't think up ten good reasons why I should not go that day. Exercise becomes fun as well as beneficial to me. And experiences that are fun and at the same time bring results are easily repeated.

I am exhilarated when the pounds begin to vanish. Organization, like exercise, can be both a discipline and a fun activity.

PREPARATION

The key word to organization is *preparation*. Webster defines *preparation* as "the process of getting ready for a specific purpose or occasion." What events do we prepare for? Weddings, anniversaries, the arrival of a newborn baby—the Big Events.

But we don't prepare for breakfast, which comes every morning, rain or shine, and laundry and marketing, which must be done every week. That's all wrong. Preparation is a key element to every activity.

10 REASONS TO ORGANIZE!

1. *You will have time to enjoy life.* You will know how to schedule personal time for just yourself, whether it is an evening art class or an hour of reading.

2. *Your physical and mental health will improve.* You will have a confident attitude. You won't have the guilt of procrastination, the stress of time pressure, or the anxiety of mismanagement. Erma Bombeck says, "I don't have stress, but I'm sure I am a carrier." The pressure points that create stress are eliminated when a person is organized.

3. *You will be in control of both big and little things.* Whether it's a large wedding six months from now or a backyard barbecue next Saturday, you will have a plan for making sure that everything comes together on schedule.

4. *You can say "No" without feeling guilty.* You will know what your obligations and commitments are months in advance. With such information at hand, you can decline additional requests and explain why you must say no for now.

5. *Your life can become less complicated.* Organized closets, purses, cupboards, and laundry rooms will save you steps, energy, needless repetition, and frustration.

6. *You can be a caring person.* You will not only have a system for remembering birthdays and anniversaries, but also the time to send cards and do things for friends and neighbors.

7. *You can save money.* A disciplined budget and a dependable recordkeeping system will allow you to control cash flow and take advantage of sales.

8. *You can reach goals.* You will become task-oriented and accomplishment-minded. You will make daily progress on projects and finish what you do.

9. *You can make wise choices.* A home or business that is under control serves as a comfort and support during times of challenge, career redirection, and uncertainty.

10. *You can please others.* Your husband will praise you for meals served on time and your children will appreciate your being able to attend their sports events and activities at school.

We elect a president in November. Yet by constitutional law he doesn't take office until January. Now I admit more preparation is needed for this high office than a couple of months, but obviously our founding fathers knew these months were necessary to prepare a smooth transition between outgoing and incoming presidents and their staffs. In every walk of life we see preparation as a key element.

We have accepted this concept for the office, for the club or service organization, but not for our homes and neighborhoods. That is a serious oversight. I feel we need to organize everything in our lives so that we can be prepared for both large and small tasks.

Good preparation is rising in the morning knowing what you are going to serve your family for breakfast, lunch, and dinner that day. A woman who is prepared is confident. She is not afraid to face the future, not only in her work, but in the day-to-day occurrences of her personal and family life. Throughout this book I will be suggesting how you can be better prepared.

SPACE AND PLACE

When I speak to a group of church women, I often read the following memo. The women look at each other as if to say, "Where's this weirdo coming from?" But I assure you this memo has more to do with organization than you might think.

> TO: Jesus, Son of Joseph
> Woodcrafter's Carpenter Shop
> Nazareth 25922
>
> FROM: Jordan Management Consultants
> Jerusalem 26544
> (Via Dr. Dryan Crenshaw,
> Greenville, SC USA)

Dear Sir:

Thank you for submitting the résumés of the 12 men you have picked for managerial positions in your new organization. All of them have now taken our battery of tests, and we have not only run the results through our computer, but also arranged personal interviews for each of them with our psychologist and vocational aptitude consultant.

It is the staff opinion that most of your nominees are lacking in background, education, and vocational aptitude for the type of enterprise you are undertaking. They do not have the team concept. We would recommend that you continue your search for persons of experience in managerial ability and proven capacity.

Simon Peter is emotionally unstable and given to fits of temper. Andrew has absolutely no qualities of leadership. The two brothers, James and John, the sons of Zebedee, place personal interest above company loyalty. Thomas demonstrates a questioning attitude that would tend to undermine morale. We feel that it is our duty to tell you that Matthew has been blacklisted by the Greater Jerusalem Better Business Bureau. James, the son of Alphaeus, and Thaddaeus definitely have radical leanings, and they both registered a high score on the manic-depressive scale.

One of the candidates, however, shows great potential. He is a man of ability and resourcefulness, meets people well, has a keen business mind, and has contacts in high places. He is highly motivated, ambitious, and responsible. We recommend Judas Iscariot as your comptroller and right-hand man. All of the other profiles are self-explanatory.

We wish you every success in your new venture.

Sincerely yours . . .

If you are a Christian, you believe that Jesus, the son of Joseph, was the Son of God. If you are Jewish, you probably believe that Christ was a wise prophet who had a great impact on man. If you are an agnostic, you will probably admit that this one man and his small band of followers began a movement that has grown and endured for almost 2000 years. Not a bad organizational accomplishment.

I realized an important concept when I first read this memo. If the God of the universe could have chosen 11 of the most unlikely men to carry out a task that changed the world, I am convinced that the same God has given me the right husband, the right house (it's not too small, it's not too big), the right child (she's not too slow, she's not too fast; she's not too fat, she's not too thin), and the very best situation for who I am and who He wants me to be. I am further convinced that I can live an orderly life. I am content with my space and place.

If I am content with my space and place, I can move forward to organize the things about me. But when I am thinking to myself, *If I had a husband who pulled the chair out for me, I could be happy,* or *If my husband only . . .,* I am too busy fretting over my imaginary or real difficulties to find time to organize my life.

Some years ago I went through a period of self-doubt. I became preoccupied with my problems. I opened my Bible to find some help and guidance. As I read, I came upon the following words, written by the apostle Paul: "But this one thing I do, forgetting those things which are behind and reaching forward to those things which are ahead, I press toward the goal for the prize" (Philippians 3:13,14).

The three steps I needed to take were suddenly laid out in proper order:

- ◆ Forget
- ◆ Reach forward
- ◆ Press on

Instead of fretting over the past, I was to forget those problems and begin to concentrate on the future and press toward my new goals.

Sounds good, doesn't it? A little too good maybe? Too much has happened to some of us, the bruises are too deep, the disappointments too great, the failures too many. How can we forget the past and be content?

A good starting place is to apply what I call "The Sponge Cake Principle" to those difficult situations, so that you can press on to new possibilities.

Edith Schaeffer, author and wife of Dr. Francis Schaeffer, tells a story about a sponge cake in her book *Hidden Art*. She and her late husband founded L'Abri, a community in Switzerland dedicated to Christian study. Each person who joined the community for a month or a couple of months or a year took part in the cleaning, cooking, and yard work.

One year a young woman named Laurie, who had been raised in a home where her mom did all the cooking and housework, came to L'Abri. The first couple of weeks she did housekeeping and gardening duties, and everything went quite well. The third week Laurie was assigned kitchen duty. Mrs Schaeffer went through all the recipes with her, since Laurie was quite nervous about cooking for 40 people The first and second days went well.

The dessert recipe for the evening meal of the third day was sponge cake and strawberries. If you have ever made sponge cake (often known as angel food cake), you know how hard the recipe is for a beginner. Laurie put the ingredients into a big bowl and mixed them. The recipe said she should have a light, frothy batter. Instead, the dough in her bowl was a yellow, sticky, gooey mess. She reread the directions: 1½ cups sugar, 1 cup cake flour, 1¼ cups egg whites. Uh, oh. She'd thrown whole eggs into the batter.

I'm just going to throw this away and start over again, she thought. *It's of no use. It can never be used again.* Then she remembered that the community ran on a very tight budget. She decided to call Mrs. Schaeffer.

"Wait a minute," Edith Schaeffer said once Laurie had told her the story and was picking up the bowl to head for the garbage. "Let's think." After a few minutes Edith added some flour to the bowl, whipped it in, added some more flour, whipped that in. Finally she threw the batter onto the floured counter and rolled it out very thin. She put weights on all four corners and let the dough dry. Later she cut it up into small strips. *Voila!* The sponge cake became home-made noodles for that night's dinner.

We have all failed sometime in our lives, as Laurie did. Many of us have faced traumatic incidents. A death. A divorce. A word spoken in haste to a friend that destroyed a relationship. But nothing can stop us from moving ahead with life. We may never be a "sponge cake," but home-made noodles are just as good and very useful. We are unique individuals. We can find peace with our space and place.

I don't know you. I don't know how you feel now or what problems you have experienced. I don't know why you are where you are or what mistakes you have made. I can't see the joy or sadness in your eyes. I would like to sit face-to-face with you, to cry with you and encourage you. I would like to be able to personally affirm you as you take these three steps: *forget, reach forward, press on.* While that is impossible, it is possible for me to say, "Don't quit! Truly, there is a new future ahead for you."

When Winston Churchill was very elderly, he was asked to return to Harrow, the public school he attended as a boy. The headmaster asked Mr. Churchill to deliver a speech to the students on the secret of success. When the day arrived, Mr. Churchill stood before the assembly and delivered a speech that was only 15 words long. He said, "Young men, never give up. Never give up! Never give up! Never, never, never, never!"

I offer the same advice to you. A space and place is reserved just for you in this world. It is yours. You are there.

Find satisfaction in it. Believe that it is a place where you can grow and change and expand. Forget the past. Reach for the good things God has in your future. Press toward your prize.

FIRST AND FAST

Now, you may be thinking that this crazy Otto woman plans to work you to death, that she wants to run you ragged every day trying to accomplish the work of ten women. Actually, nothing could be further from the truth. Whereas, yes, I do want you to be a disciplined and organized worker, I want you to do it to *save* energy and *retain* your pep rather than squander your strength.

Do you know what really makes you tired? *The things you don't do, not the things you do!*

Think of a project, large or small, that you delayed over and over again. You needed to exert mental, physical, emotional energy, and maybe even stretch the family finances to accomplish it. That project sat like a heavy weight on both of your shoulders. But once you went ahead and exerted the energy, you felt terrific. You don't agree? Let me illustrate.

Remember the last time you went out and worked in the yard all day? You pulled weeds, mowed the lawn, and got your children to clip the hedges. You took a big plastic bag and finally retrieved the McDonald's cup from behind the shrub, the old wet newspapers from the end of the driveway, and the twigs near the house. "Whew!" you say. But there's more. You swept out the garbage, made the children wash the car, and waved at your husband perched high on a ladder washing the bedroom windows.

How did you feel at the end of that day? Sore, maybe. Ready for a hot bath and a glass of iced tea, maybe. But not as tired mentally or physically as you sometimes feel at the end of a day in which you accomplish very little. And how nice it was to get up the next day and view your yard all tidy and well manicured.

Procrastination—worrying about the things you need to get done, putting them off because you dread them or because you would rather be doing something else—makes you tired, not work.

Your creative thinking is held hostage, overtaken by a need to keep everything running and the necessity to find enough hours to complete all the routine obligations. Your positive attitude deteriorates. You begin to focus on the fact that no one appreciates all you do or understands how busy you are. No one seems to care whether or not you ever get a few minutes alone without another load of wash calling for your immediate attention. Your body feels tired, just from the strain of knowing there are so many things you should do that you never will get to.

Believe me, I know how you feel. I've been there. Even now, there are things in my life that I hate to think about tackling. Yet, putting them off only wearies me. For instance, I have Mexican tile in my home, which is very common in Arizona and basically requires very little maintenance. Twice a year, however, like it or not, the tile requires treatment. And this is not a 30-minute task. Try one day and a lot of elbow grease. The furniture must be moved completely out of the area. Rugs have to be rolled up and dragged to the hall. Our family routine gets set back a day, and no visitors are allowed.

I use any excuse I can find to avoid this job. But every day I put it off, it becomes a greater burden. Each morning I see Mexican tile in my mind as I wake up. I feel guilty when I open my daybook and see the words *Clean the tile* written on my to-do list. Finally, sick of thinking about the job, I call the family together and say, "Okay, this is it! On Saturday, it's all hands on deck."

Once the ordeal is over, I feel great. I determine that I won't procrastinate again. And guess what? I am finally getting better. I've adopted "first and fast," a slogan I originally created for my daughter, as my new motto.

When Anissa was a little girl, she would eat all around the foods she didn't like, then pull the "I'm full" routine on me. I soon devised the "first and fast" approach. I convinced her it was much easier to eat foods she disliked first, to get them quickly out of the way, than to leave them until the last. After all, what taste remains in your mouth after dinner?

Now I apply this approach to household chores I dislike, to telephone calls I don't want to make. And it works. Women in my classes who have adopted the "first and fast" principle often call to tell me how applicable it is to all areas of their lives: their own personal endeavors, their children's problems, their employees' work. Try it and find out for yourself.

Two Vital Organizational Attributes

Sensitivity. Some people may be too sensitive, but I have never met anyone with too much sensitivity. Let me say that another way so you will know exactly what I mean. Some people may be too conscious of their own faults or how people interact with them, but no one can be too sensitive to other people's needs. I may be particularly aware of this because some very special, sensitive people have had a profound influence on my life.

As a child, I thought Mrs. Erich, my seventh grade homeroom teacher and a tall, gray-headed, thin woman, was a little aloof. Now I realize she was a woman who was sensitive to the needs of her students, especially one skinny girl, Donna Centanne, who, at that point, had few positive physical or personality attributes.

Psychologists tell us that pretty children get the most attention in class. I certainly did not fall into that category. I was about 5'4" tall, weighed about 89 pounds, and wore clothes that were very plain. Somehow Mrs. Erich saw something in me that no one else could see. When I went into eighth grade, the school was forced to divide our class into two classes because the enrollment had grown. Most of the class stayed together in an eighth grade classroom, the rest of us were put into a class with seventh-grade students.

This overflow classroom was not the best learning environment, especially for that impetuous Centanne kid. I quickly linked up with four young girls who shared my exuberant personality. We went everywhere as a group: to classes, to lunch, to recess, and even places after school. No one could separate us—except Mrs. Erich.

She saw something in the other four girls that didn't please her. And she saw a change in the Donna Centanne she had taught in seventh grade. She quickly pulled strings to have me transferred out of the overflow classroom and put back into the contained eighth-grade class.

I thought my whole world had come to an end. What would I do without my new buddies? How would I ever fit in with this new bunch of kids?

Little did I know that Mrs. Erich had decided to help me make something of myself. Those four girls all found themselves in unfortunate situations by the time they were 30 years old, as Mrs. Erich suspected. However, the new girls with whom I made friends in the eighth grade are still my friends to this day. I like to think that I honor my seventh-grade teacher each time I show concern for other women and teach them how to become orderly so they can reach out to others, as she did to me.

Part of sensitivity is being in touch with yourself. Know when you are too busy, when you are tired, when you are irritable. Schedule some easier and quieter days if you can. Take an hour or two to unwind. As you do this, you'll become more sensitive to the schedules of your family members.

The moments alone together, the gentle touch, the "I love you's"—both spoken and unspoken—have made David and me very best friends. When Anissa seems to have too much to do, I try to slow her activities down. "No, I don't think you should stay overnight with Sarah tonight. You were at Ruthie's house last night." When she is bored, I try to suggest a physical activity, from swimming to housework. Sensitivity is a vital organizational attribute. Every once in a while, the first priority on my daily to-do list is "Be more sensitive."

Enthusiasm. There is nothing more contagious than enthusiasm. It spreads like wildfire. We are all contagious, and we choose what we want to spread to our families and friends.

You don't choose to be contagious; you simply are! But you do choose what you spread.

Is it joy and enthusiasm or negativism?

I affect the lives of everyone I know when I infect them with a shot of enthusiasm. The old song, "Smile and the world smiles with you, cry and you cry alone," is only half true. "Cry and the world cries with you" is a truer reflection of life.

An acquaintance of mine took the reins of a downtrodden Parent/Teacher Association, which was riddled with negativism. Led by her enthusiastic "We will succeed" attitude, the group raised $10,000 in one year, purchased playground equipment, and revived the spirit of the organization. Several people remarked at year's end, "Her contagious enthusiasm carried over to each of us." In an appreciation ceremony, the principal said, "Enthusiasm accomplished this feat!"

It works! Try it!

AN ORGANIZER/PLANNER

For the last 25 years I have carried an expandable notebook, which I finally called my "daybook." I am firmly convinced that this tool, more than all of the other organizational tools, will be your most valuable.

That's why, after we talk about the importance of bringing your life into clearer focus, I am going to show you how to create a daybook that is perfect for *you*. I will give you ideas for everything from budgeting to keeping track of your wardrobe. I'll show you how to use simple forms that will help you organize your life. If you are among the many women who already own a commercially prepared planner but have never been able to understand it or use it to its fullest potential, the next several chapters are for you! They will prove invaluable in helping you unlock your planner's secrets. If you have never taken the step to an organizer/planner, I've enclosed a complete series of blank forms at the end of this book, which can be enlarged or reduced on a photocopier for your own use.* Feel free to use these samples as they are, or as a starting point for creating your own customized forms. Add, subtract, mix, and match forms to suit your lifestyle. Whether the forms are copied, printed, or even handwritten, the goal of a daybook is to have an organized place to keep all of your thoughts in order.

Once an organizer/planner becomes your memory, you will find relief from having to keep track of everything in your mind. The daybook will become a central data center, holding all the information that will make your life run smoothly and efficiently. Discipline yourself to use your daybook constantly. If the book is always with you, you will be able to write down all your ideas and goals, no matter when or where you think of them. If you are like me, your best ideas don't come at your desk, but rather in the car or at the park.

---

* If you prefer, you can order many of these preprinted forms directly from me. For more information, see the last page of this book

A FINAL WORD

You can be organized. You can bring your life under control. No matter who you are, no matter how disorganized you appear to be, you can do it. Start slowly. Take one step at a time.

I am excited about what is going to happen in your life. Time management consultant Alan Lakein puts it this way: "Time is life. It is irreversible and irreplaceable. To waste your time is to waste your life, but to master your time is to master your life and make the most of it."

As we set out together on this journey, we will first look at the importance of setting goals. Then we will discover how to use your daybook to set your mind free from the details of life that all too often weigh you down. Finally, we will go beyond your daybook to see how incorporating some simple organizational activities into your home and personal routines will help you enjoy life to its fullest!

3

Bring Your Life into Focus

My friend Sally met Mr. Knight-in-Shining-Armor one year after she graduated from high school. Her family didn't like him very much, but this only increased her desire to "show them." Sally's main goal in life was to have a good marriage. Her parents had been divorced when she was young, and she vowed it would never happen to her.

She married Mr. Knight-in-Shining-Armor when she was 19 years old and set out to fulfill her goal. After six months of marriage she discovered that her husband was having an affair. I was with her the afternoon she found out. She held her stomach and cried, "The pain is so, so deep. Will I ever recover?"

Still, Sally held on to her goal. She forgave her husband and did everything she could to please him. For the next five years, I watched her suffer the turmoil of living with an alcoholic husband who physically abused her and emotionally robbed her of dignity. With each new affair, Sally asked herself, *What am I doing wrong that he has to have other women?* One evening she called from a phone booth. "Will you come and get me?" she asked. "I can't take it anymore."

As I turned into Sally's street I saw her sitting on her bicycle in her nightgown under the street light. Her hair was tousled and black streaks from her mascara streamed down her face. Later, at my house, I discovered a bald spot on the top of her head where her husband had literally pulled her hair out by flinging her across the room by her hair.

Still, Sally refused to leave the man. Her goal was to have a good marriage, and she doggedly pursued it. Two years later her husband announced that his latest girl was divorcing her husband. "Get out," he announced. "I'm filing for divorce too. She and I are going to get married."

Sally was heartbroken. She had failed at her greatest desire and goal: to have a happy marriage.

My friend Sally is all too typical of many other women who think their desires can also be their goals in life.

GOALS VS. DESIRES

"Do you know the difference between a goal and a desire?" I often ask the women in my seminars.

"Sure," someone replies. "A goal is a desire written down. It's a New Year's resolution that is acted upon."

Unfortunately, that's what many people, like my friend Sally, think. They confuse or interchange the words *goal* and *desire*, but the two are not the same. A goal is something I can accomplish. I, alone, under God's control, exclusive of anyone else, can make this happen. A desire, however, is something that I have no control over because it most often involves someone or something else.

Can a good marriage be one of my goals? Many women answer yes. Having a good marriage is, in fact, one of their goals. No wonder many women become so disillusioned when they can't reach that goal. Having a good marriage is *not* a goal. It is a desire. I, alone, cannot have a good marriage. No matter what kind of wife I choose to be, if my husband decides to be uncooperative, a good marriage is out of reach.

You can see why realistic goal setting is so important. Sometimes we cannot reach the goals we set. Why? Not because we have not tried, but because we have set goals that are really desires. What is my goal in marriage? To be a good wife. This is something I can accomplish exclusive of David.

This concept, developed by psychologist Larry Crabb, helped me to set realistic goals. A goal is:

+ an objective *I* can accomplish

+ an objective *I* want to see happen in my life.

+ an objective over which *I* have complete control.

I have a friend, Jane, who is overweight. One of my goals cannot be: I would like Jane to lose weight this year. That is my desire for her, but it has to be her goal. I can support her—I can encourage her to take an aerobics class with me—but she has to accomplish the task.

Now you take it from there. Look at your own wants and desires. Are your desires and goals mixed together? Perhaps this is why you are having trouble accomplishing some of the things you thought were goals. Separate your desires from your goals and start again. I assure you, you will have greater success.

I often ask the women in my seminars another question. "How many of you have goals?" Hands wave everywhere. Ninety percent or more indicate they have goals. Then I ask, "How many of you have written them down?" Hands go down, people start twisting their rings or plowing through their purses for a breath mint or handkerchief. Only about a tenth of the women have actually written their goals down.

I think we are afraid to write our goals down on paper, since putting them in black and white commits us to action. Yet it is very important that we write goals down, because 80 percent of the people who write their goals down accomplish them. Conversely, only 20 percent of those who do not write their goals actually achieve them.

YOUR OVERALL PURPOSE

Your most important task in the goal-setting process is to determine your overall purpose in life. Once you determine your life goal, you will then know how to establish short-term goals that will help you fulfill this role.

Have you ever wandered through an old graveyard? If you have, I imagine you have been fascinated with the epitaphs written on the headstones. Years ago, an epitaph—a phrase of ten or fewer words that summed up the impact of that person's life—was as important a part of the gravestone information as the person's name and lifespan dates. Sometimes a person wrote the epitaph himself. Other times a relative or loved one summarized that person's life.

As you think about your life goal, or "Life Phrase," think about how you would like to be remembered by your family, friends, and business associates. What impact would you like to have on those around you? You should be able to state your Life Phrase in about ten words.

Coming up with a Life Phrase will not be as easy as it may seem to you as you read this. Go slowly. Take a week to ten days to think about what you truly want out of life for yourself and what you wish to contribute to the lives of others. Don't plan to sit down in one hour and write your Life Phrase. You will only be frustrated.

Keep a piece of paper or a notepad with you during the next few weeks. As you are washing dishes or cleaning, ask yourself, "How do I want to be remembered? What do I want my unique contribution to my family, my friends, my neighbors, and those around me to be?"

If a word comes to mind, write it down. If you come up with a phrase, write that down. Don't worry if the words or phrases connect in any way. Just capture them on paper so you won't forget. The word *enthusiasm* was one of the first words that came to me, along with *example* and *joy*. I didn't put my Life Phrase together for another couple of weeks afterward. I thought about the words and phrases I had written, I prayed about them, and finally I wrote a complete phrase: "To share the joy of my life with others through my enthusiasm, examples, teaching, actions, and perseverance." (Okay, so I did go over the ten-word limit. But you get the idea.)

Each year I review that phrase to make sure it's still my purpose in life. Eighteen years later, I don't want to change a single word, but I might someday in the future.

SPECIFIC GOALS

Having decided upon a Life Phrase, the next step is to develop a series of supportive goals that will put you on target to fulfill your life goal. Most of your goals will fall into one of these eight areas: social, emotional, physical, intellectual, spiritual, family, career, or miscellaneous.

Take eight pieces of paper, one for each of the eight areas. Begin to jot down ideas in each category. Again, don't worry about complete sentences, just write words or phrases. Take a week or so to mull over the ideas, and then write them into actual sentences.

Your goals might look something like this:

> ◆ Intellectual: To further my education by taking a class or studying by myself at home.

> ◆ Physical: To exercise.
> To lose weight.

- ✦ Emotional: To control my temper.
- ✦ Financial: To save money this year.
- ✦ Social: To increase my social activity. To relax more.
- ✦ Spiritual: To devote more time to prayer and Bible study.
- ✦ Family: To be a good wife and mother.
- ✦ Career: To improve my speaking and writing.
- ✦ Miscellaneous: To finish the decoration of my master bedroom.

Once these general goals are established, you should write out specific goals that will insure that you succeed at each objective. These goals must be specific and detailed, point-blank and directed, functional and pragmatic. Note how the above goals can lead from general statements to practical and systematic procedures:

- ✦ Intellectual: To further my education by taking a class or studying by myself at home. *I will finish reading Sandburg's* Lincoln. *I will take an art history class this fall.*
- ✦ Physical: To exercise. To lose weight. *I will enroll in a water aerobics class that meets three times a week.*
- ✦ Emotional: To control my temper. *I will stop and count to five before I answer someone with an angry remark. I will apologize if I don't.*

◆ Financial: To save money this year.

I will save $3000 this year by creating a year's budget and keeping an accurate record of my expenses on the Household Budget form in my daybook.

◆ Social: To increase my social activity. To relax more.

I will invite friends over for a special occasion once a month.

I will read the Bombeck article, "If I Had My Life to Live Over," once a month. I will read Tim Hansel's book When I Relax I Feel Guilty?

◆ Spiritual: To devote more time to prayer and Bible study.

I will study the book of James.

I will get up early and spend one half-hour in Bible reading and prayer each day.

◆ Family: To be a good wife and mother.

I will prepare one of my husband's favorite meals on Sundays.

I will spend two hours each week in private time with my daughter this year.

◆ Career: To improve my speaking and writing.

I will develop major themes in my life for retreat engagements.

◆ Miscellaneous:　To finish the decoration of my master bedroom.
I will make a quilt of a famous design for our bed.

Now you can check each of these goals against this five-point test:

1. Do I have complete control over this goal?

2. Will I take full responsibility for this goal?

3. Am I willing to accomplish the goal? Will I hold onto it, despite any obstacles?

4. Is it possible for me to achieve this goal, recognizing my own limits and capabilities?

5. Have I considered what it will cost me to achieve this goal?

Thought and commitment go into goal setting, as you can see. Goals cannot be made like New Year's resolutions. I begin to develop my own goals for the coming year in the fall. I look at my current goals and how my own growth has either been enhanced this year or stunted. I then think about next year's goals. What might the next year bring? Are there any changes in my life that I know in advance will take place then? Often I have a phrase or word that sums up my yearly goal. In 1993, it was "repeat, repeat, repeat!"

My goals are never set in concrete, but they do become firm by December. By the time New Year's Eve gets here, I know where I'm going for the next year. Do you?

I have taken all this time to talk about yearly goals. I also make five-year goals. My five-year goals are:

◆ To continue making time for hikes with David.

◆ To maintain my weight between 128 and 135 pounds.

◆ To maintain good physical posture.

◆ To read the Bible through completely each year.

Having a long-range view of my life gives me perspective on the present and optimism for future years.

TEMPORARY GOALS

Let me explain one more set of goals. They are optional, but can be helpful as you begin to organize your life. I call them temporary goals. These goals can be seasonal, related to holidays like Christmas, or they can be goals you set for yourself to accomplish while your husband and children are out of town for a week. What a special time to finish projects, like painting the kitchen or spending extra time in the sewing room or catching up on your correspondence!

I often set temporary summer goals: Clean the patio or redo the family photo albums. All the times of your life can be useful and productive if you will just take the time to establish written goals and then follow through on them. Redeem the time! Don't waste it.

PUTTING YOUR GOALS INTO ACTION

Once I am satisfied with my goals, I use the exercise in personal goals to plan the steps I need to take to achieve these goals. (See Form 1 at the end of this chapter. You might want to copy this page several times over for your own use.) For instance, I will save $3000 this year by creating a year's budget and keeping an accurate record of my expenses on the household budget form in my daybook.

What must *I* do to accomplish this goal?

1. I will record a year of our family's expenses.

2. I will consider the areas that seem extravagant and can be cut. I will find at least $1500 that can be eliminated.

3. I will establish a realistic budget for next year.

4. I will monitor this budget each month by using the household budget form in my daybook.

5. I will put $167 per month in the bank.

Some of your goals may not need extensive planning; for example: "I will stop and count to five before I answer someone with an angry remark. I will apologize if I don't." Please do not be intimidated by the number of steps involved in the goal-setting process. If you only set three goals and you carry those goals through to completion in the next year, that's fine. It is much better than setting too many goals and becoming frustrated because you cannot achieve them. Remember, success breeds success, failure breeds failure.

Read your goals regularly. Check your progress. And don't be afraid to change some or update your goals—or eventually even laugh at a few of them. As I said in chapter 2, you are not the same person today that you were last year. In six months you will be different from who you now are. Goals must be as flexible as you are. Even if your Life Phrase remains constant, your ways of fulfilling that goal may alter or expand; so your supportive goals must be able to adapt to changing times.

I am still learning that fun and relaxation should be on my goal list. After I made reading the Erma Bombeck article, "If I Had My Life to Live Over," once a month a goal, I photocopied the article and put it in my daybook.

In the article Erma said, "Someone asked me the other day if I had my life to live over would I change anything?"

At first she answered no. Then she thought about it and changed her mind. Reading her list of "If I had my life to live over I would have..." often helps me to avoid being too busy, which is my natural tendency. For instance, Erma says, "When my child kissed me impetuously, I would never have said, 'Later. Now go get washed up for dinner.'" And, "I would have cried and laughed less while watching television... and more while watching real life."

I am learning to remember that there are times when it is all right to put up our feet, chat with friends, picnic with our families, take a drive just for the fun of it, or read an entertaining book. I take time to smell the roses.

A PLANNING DAY

If you are married I highly recommend that you and your husband take a day away from home for goal setting and planning. David and I get away every other month for "planning hikes." We take our backpacks full of food, our daybooks, and our Bibles and head out alone to the mountains near Scottsdale. During this time, we plan our schedules, talk about the things we want to accomplish as a couple *and* as a family, and discuss areas we need to work on in our marriage. We talk about the personal goals that seem most difficult to us, and we offer support to each other so we can make it easier for the other person to achieve his or her goals. It's a great way for you and your husband to begin to separate the urgent from the important. Sometimes I use these few paragraphs from an article entitled "The Tyranny of the Urgent" by Charles E. Hummel to help me do exactly that:

> When we stop to evaluate, we realize that our dilemma goes deeper than shortage of time; it is basically the problem of priorities. We live in constant tension between the urgent and the important. The problem is that the important task rarely must be done today or even this

week. . . . But the urgent tasks call for instant action—endless demands, pressure every hour and day. When you take inventory and plan your days, it provides fresh perspective on your work. . . . The way [becomes] clear.

Maybe you're more the Hilton than the backpacking type. Perhaps you could find someone to watch the children so you and your husband could spend the day at home together. You don't have to have a certain set of surroundings, but you do need to be alone. Talk about your goals, about who you are as individuals and who you are as husband and wife. As a wife, I find submission easier when I know David's heart and goals in specific areas. Share some of your personal needs. Create common goals for your marriage, but define your individual directions as mother and father.

Naturally, even though you will be sharing ideas and thoughts and plans with your spouse, you will also need time by yourself for personal goal setting.

ESTABLISHING PRIORITIES

Now that you have a Life Phrase and your goals all written down, and you have placed them in your daybook and you're going to review them every so often, your life has become organized. Right? *Wrong.* You've still got to make your Life Phrase and goals a part of your everyday decision-making process.

This is where priorities come in. Establishing priorities forces us to rate our choices: "I shall do this rather than that." Unfortunately, too many of us just say yes to most activities. If you are like me, a woman who likes to do *everything*, establishing priorities can be especially difficult. For me, *everything* was important and at the top of my agenda. Listing my priorities helped me learn to say no.

A number of years ago I met an older woman at a church meeting. She wasn't beautiful, but she looked extremely attractive in a tailored gray suit. She talked to me about her family and asked me questions about my family, my interests, and my desires.

In the next weeks and months, as I began to know her better, I was even more impressed. She cared for the needs of her family and still managed to serve on the school board and participate in a church women's group. One day I asked this lady how she managed to look so well dressed, accomplish so much, and still seem so relaxed and full of joy.

"I have learned to ask myself a very important question before adding any activity to my life. The question is: Can someone else do it?"

At first I didn't understand what she was saying, and I told her so.

"There are three, four, maybe five things in life that only I can do," she explained. "Those things come first. Everything else is optional."

I experimented with this concept in my life, and I discovered that it really works. It helped me both to define my priorities and lock in on them so no one could sway me off target.

Whenever anyone asks me to take on a new task, a new responsibility or obligation, I first ask myself, "Can somebody else do it?" If the answer is yes, I ask myself, "Am I meeting my priorities?"

I like to speak on life management, and I feel called to speak. Can anybody else do that? Yes. I like to teach Cub Scouts. Can anybody else do that? Yes, you bet they can. Can anyone else be David's wife? No. I'm the only one who can do that.

I have not stopped speaking to women's groups, but I only accept engagements when they don't infringe upon the things that I alone can do. I stay loyal to my priorities.

What are these priorities? What are those things that only Donna Otto can do? Not many in number, just as my friend said, but each a weighty and serious responsibility.

- ◆ I alone am responsible for my relationship to God.

- ◆ I alone am responsible for who I am. I have to provide myself with the intellectual and spiritual stimulation to become all that I can be.

- ◆ I alone can be David Otto's wife. Other people will be his friends, his colleagues, his teachers, but I am the only one who can love and care for him as his wife.

- ◆ I alone can be Anissa Otto's mother. Other people will influence her life, but only I can give her a mother's love and care and thereby fulfill my responsibility to her.

- ◆ I alone can manage my household. I might have a housekeeper or a husband who helps around the house. Nevertheless, I am ultimately responsible for managing my household.

These five things can only be done by Donna Otto. They are my priorities. What are yours? Take a moment now to write them on a sheet of paper. You may be an only child, so the care of an aging parent might be one of your priorities.

Now make them a part of your life. Keep them in the back of your mind as you go through your day. Write them on a page in your daybook.

A few years ago I was getting ready to teach a Christmas class. I was in the center of—or had actually become—a whirlwind. I still had to finalize the seminar outline, get the handouts ready, and make 300 name tags. Late in the afternoon Anissa burst through the door into our dining room, which I had purposely shut because the partly finished name tags and the colored paper were strewn all over the table, and asked, "What's for dinner, Mom?"

"Dinner!" I said, my glue-covered finger sticking to the latest name tag. "I've got name tags to make for 300 women!"

I still remember the look on her face.

I finished the name tags. Anissa made her own dinner that night. Yes, I blew it. It wasn't the first time and it probably won't be the last. But now I've learned to ask the question: Can someone else do it? Taking the time to do that allows me the space to put my priorities in order. Believe me, the next year I decided not to make name tags for my Christmas seminar.

If you must work outside the home, then that, of course, becomes one of your priorities. If you are working by choice, and it interferes with the keeping of your priorities, perhaps you should reexamine that decision. Some women tell me that after looking carefully at their priorities, they discover their reason for working is to accumulate more material wealth. In the process they find they have been sacrificing the important responsibilities of being a good wife and mother and growing in Christ. Knowing, in this day and age, the delicacy of this subject, I offer these thoughts to provoke and stimulate your thinking, not to judge you.

COMMITMENT AND VISION

Cost is an important factor in any decision. How often have you refused to buy a lovely silk blouse because it cost $50? To get ahead on the job we must often pay the price of working extra hours or handling a load of paperwork at home without extra pay. But when it comes to reaching our personal goals—making those improvements that we know need to be made—we often, in childlike fashion, want something to happen without having to pay the price.

To achieve a goal we must often change, which involves sacrifice and discipline. Writing down goals takes *commitment*—and *vision*.

Often children fail to reach their goals because they lose their vision of accomplishment. A little girl will say, "Mommy, let's put my 500-piece puzzle together." The finished picture on the box top inspires and excites the child. *I will have a neat picture like that to show my friends*, she thinks. After a half-hour of hunting through 500 interlocking pieces for just the right one to fit with another, however, the child grows weary. She asks permission to go do something else. She no longer has the vision of a completed puzzle, so she fails at her original goal.

A similar situation occurred to Florence Chadwick, who was the first woman to swim the English Channel in both directions. After this record-setting feat, she tried to swim the 21 miles from Catalina Island to the California coast. Millions of people were watching on television.

The fog was so thick she could hardly see the boats that were protecting her. Sharks came very close. Fatigue had never been a problem for her, but the Catalina water was so very cold she became numb after about 15 hours. She could not go on. Her mother and her trainer, who were in the boat beside her, kept telling her that land was just ahead. "Don't quit," they yelled over and over again. But Florence could not see the California coast. The blanket of fog obscured her vision.

After 15 hours and 55 minutes, Florence Chadwick was taken out of the water. When she began to recover her senses several hours later and realized her failure, she told a reporter, "Look, I'm not excusing myself. But if I could have seen the land, I might have made it." She had given up when the California coast was only a half mile away. "I was licked by the fog—not fatigue," she said. The fog obscured her vision of achievement.

Two months later Florence Chadwick swam the same channel. Again the fog obscured her view, but this time she kept her mental vision of the land ahead. She became the first woman to swim the Catalina Channel, beating the men's record by nearly two hours. Commitment and vision are necessary to achieve any goal. Never lose your vision of your Life Phrase, your goals, and your priorities.

If you lived in Chicago and you and your family decided to vacation by driving across the country to California, you would get a map, chart a course, follow it, and wind up at your destination within a specific amount of time. If you drove the same course without a map, the trip would be a disaster. You would meander and stray all over the country in haphazard fashion until you finally fell into the Grand Canyon and no one would ever hear from you again.

By writing down a Life Phrase for yourself and developing support goals to operate by, you are symbolically creating a map for your life With the help of a map, you will reach your destinations.

Exercise in Personal Goals

Name _____

A goal of mine is:

_____

_____

What must *I* do to accomplish this goal?	Date begun:	Target date:	Complete date:
	_____	_____	_____

Steps:

1) _____

2) _____

3) _____

4) _____

5) _____

6) _____

Notes regarding my goals: How did I set this goal? Why did I set this goal? What purpose will it serve in my life?

Use one sheet for each goal. Then list goals and steps with target dates in a place you can review regularly to check your progress.

Form 1

4

Your Daily Planner: A Friend for Life

E *veryone is in a hurry these days. It used to be that people were willing to wait three days for a stage-* coach. Today, they get upset if they miss one section of a revolving door or the fax is slow.

There just doesn't seem to be enough time in the day to do all that we need to do, much less any time for what we *want* to do.

Ben Franklin said, "Time is the stuff life is made of." If that's the case, most of us feel we've had the "stuffing" kicked out of us.

Personal management seems like a losing game even for the most serious-minded, goal-oriented people. Have you ever analyzed a typical year? Let's do so together.

We begin each year with 12 months .... 365 days

Most employees take off two weeks'
    annual vacation .... 351 days left

No one works on New Year's Day, Memorial
    Day, Labor Day, and five other holidays   343 days left

Eight hours of nightly sleep adds up to 122
    calendar days of no work .... 221 days left

A one-hour lunch break Monday through Friday
    equals 11 24-hour days annually . . . . 210 days left
Excluding vacation weeks, there are still 102
    weekend days when work isn't done . . . . 108 days left

Now, 108 workdays out of 365 is about a 29 percent efficiency rate. And that doesn't include time off for sick days, funerals, company seminars, and personal business days (which lower the effective work outlay to about 23 percent efficiency).

Let me ask you: Would you purchase a refrigerator that was guaranteed to work 29 percent of the time? Would you buy a ticket to fly on an airplane that was guaranteed to be 23 percent efficient and functional? Ha! Fat chance, eh? Me neither. Yet, that's the problem employers face when trying to get efficient work out of employees. And in your role as a home manager, the problem is equally as challenging, if not worse. After all, how many of *those* people are having to get up in the middle of the night to nurse an infant? How many of *them* are interrupted every five minutes by a child who needs a cracker or a toy or a hug or a storybook read out loud?

Life management seems like "Mission Impossible" for most women. They have good intentions; they always expect that "someday" they will get organized and task-oriented. Someday. For sure, someday they'll do it. I often hear: "I *really am* going to get organized. . . . Uh, just as soon as I can get the time to get around to it."

One of my friends, Mary, a wife and mother of two children, likes to talk about her "organizational fantasy." In this fantasy, everyone in the world has seven days a week, 24 hours a day. Everyone—except her. She has eight days. Very soon she becomes the only one who has everything done. Each closet in her house is clean, every drawer is neat. Every button is sewn on. She is so well-organized that her Christmas gifts are bought, wrapped, and labeled in July!

With a smile on her face, she watches her friends frantically trying to finish their spring cleaning before September.

I suppose we all have fantasies of one sort or another. What is yours? Perhaps it is the same fantasy many other women have, simply of having two or three extra hours in a day, rather than my neighbor's eight-day-week fantasy. Wouldn't that be wonderful? You could get caught up and finished with all the projects you've started but never completed.

I can see you now. You're preparing different menus for dinner, wallpapering the bathroom, spending time with each child individually, and—believe it or not—spending an hour in your room reading or doing your nails.

Sound good? Well, this scenario is as much a fantasy as my friend's extra day. Most of us would use 26 hours just the way we use 24. Having more hours does not make you organized. Making proper use of the hours does.

That is why I'm so excited about personal organization. I have seen it work in my own life. Now I want to give you some basic principles of organization that will also change your life.

A LIFETIME OF TIME

A man I know who is a doctor of linguistics told me that there are more than 40 expressions in the English language that are *excuses* for not being time efficient. If you have ever heard someone say "Time flies" or "Time goes by faster as you get older," then you know what I'm referring to.

My mother used to say, "Man works from sun to sun, but a woman's work is never done." (To which my father would say, "Spend less time reciting clichés and you'll get more accomplished, Esther.")

What all this shows us is that, to paraphrase Mark Twain, "Everybody talks about time management but nobody does anything about it."

But, guess what? For a fact, there's much you *can* do about it. By learning to use a daybook, you can start to make maximum use of your time. That's what we are going to focus on in this chapter, because I am convinced that once you start using an effective organizer and planner you will be a new person.

If you were to ask me, "Who needs to use a good organizer?" my answer would be *every woman*, whether a full-time housewife, a businesswoman, a volunteer worker, a mother, a married woman, a single woman, or a combination of all or any of these personalities. I truly believe every woman needs an organizer to bring her life and activities under control.

Did you know that most people are not able to explain in detail just how they spend their days and weeks? They just know that they are "busy" with various "activities." Try to pin these people down, however, with point-blank questions like, "How many minutes did you spend on the phone yesterday?" or "How many hours did you spend watching TV last week?" and they won't be able to tell you. They are just winging their daily schedules and handling things as they come.

Until you know how you currently spend your time, it is most difficult, in fact, nearly impossible, to reorganize. One effective way to track your activities is to use a simple form like Form 2 at the end of the chapter.

The purpose of the form is to allow you, figuratively speaking, to follow yourself around for a week. The top of the form is labeled by the days of the week. The left side of the form is divided into half-hour segments ranging from 8:00 A.M. to 5:30 P.M. You can draw a grid like this on a large piece of notebook paper or photocopy Form 2 and carry it in your daybook or purse for one week.

As you go through each day make a note of what you did during each half-hour segment. For example, on Monday from 8:00 to 8:30 A.M. you might have "made beds

& breakfast," and from 8:30 to 9:00 A.M. you may have "packed lunches/changed baby/got dressed."

Continue this practice for one week. It will make you aware of the many ways you are actually squandering time. Now tally all the time you spent on the activities evaluation (Form 3 at the end of this chapter). Consider the activities listed at the bottom of the form: sleeping, working, commuting, meal preparation (include time spent in eating), dressing and clothes preparation, watching television, etc. For instance, you slept 6 hours a night for 7 nights, a total of 42 hours. You worked a 6-hour day 5 days, a total of 30 hours. List all of your activities and then total the hours. Don't be surprised if you have 175 hours, even though there are only 168 hours in a week.

As you do this, you'll catch yourself saying, "Oh, surely, I didn't *really* spend 27½ hours watching television," and "Did I *honestly* spend more than 11 hours talking on the phone last week?" And since you will do your own tallying, you will *have* to believe the numbers.

You will also learn how to make time do double duty for you. Let's say, for example, that you are a woman who is employed outside the home from Monday through Friday. In checking your end-of-week tallies on your form you notice two interesting things: 1) you logged zero hours of "studying," and 2) you logged ten hours of weekly "traveling" because it takes you half an hour each morning to drive to work and half an hour to drive home at night. So, what do you do? You put a cassette recorder in your car and play educational tapes each day on the way to and from work. That's an hour of studying each day on how to speak French or how to improve your sales talk or how to develop a better memory or how to lose weight—or whatever interests you.

Now look at the second half of the chart. First ask yourself: "What must I do?" List those activities and their times. Next ask yourself, "With the time remaining, what do I want to do?"

Now reorganize your week. Make time for the activities you enjoy, such as tennis. Cut back on those that seem to be wasted, like watching television (remember what Erma Bombeck said) and talking on the phone. When you finish filling out the second form, you will be on your way to controlling your time. All organizational and time management problems can be solved, but first you have to discover what the problems are. You now know how to do that.

Wait a minute! I know what you're thinking: "That's too much work. I want to get organized, not fill out forms. Besides, I know pretty much how I spend my time!"

Yes, goal setting does require some work. Yes, it may even be a bother for a day or so. But if you're serious about getting a grip on your time and if you're willing to astound yourself at the amount of your time that goes for nonessentials, then go through this process. Believe me, you will be surprised! There's no other way to see where you are today.

CREATING YOUR OWN DAYBOOK

My husband and daughter often accuse me of having no memory at all. They may be right. My daybook has become my memory. When they tease me, I always answer, "All geniuses keep their minds uncluttered."

Albert Einstein didn't even know his own telephone number! He had more important priorities for his mind. His logic was, "I never memorize anything that I can easily look up."

My daybook and I are inseparable. I would no more go anywhere without it than I would go out without my wedding band or my glasses. For me, it is a necessity. I cannot function effectively without it. With it, I usually can function more effectively than two women. So can you. It truly is that remarkable.

If you like, you can start as I did many years ago with a cardboard three-ring binder. Purchase some paper that fits, make your own tabs, and experiment to see what works best for you. (Remember that old adage: "Anything will work, if you will.") If you're already using a preprinted organizer, the information in these next chapters will help you customize it to fit your lifestyle. The important thing is to develop a system you feel comfortable with—and one you will actually *use*.

I designed the forms in these chapters after years of experimenting with other organizers and after years of listening to women discuss in my classes and seminars what they felt they needed in a planner. They were created to service all the areas most women have in common, yet also to meet the unique individual facets of each woman's career and personality.

If you have important telephone numbers written on the backs of deposit slips, to-do lists scribbled on the backs of old envelopes, receipts stuffed in your pockets, grocery lists lost at the bottom of your purse, and notes stuck to your countertops with peanut butter and jelly, you are a prime candidate for a planner/organizer. You don't have to have a personality that lends itself to organization and detailing in order to make one work for you. I don't. I used to hide my dirty dishes in the clothes dryer. All you have to have is an interest in accomplishing certain things in your life. You can learn the rest.

Right about now you may want to say to me, "This all sounds good, but I don't keep records. I have never used a binder. I have never kept a journal. I am one of those people you mentioned a minute ago who uses little scraps of paper and jams them into a purse. I really like the concept; I would really like to be organized. But where do I begin?"

Very simply, you begin with two basic words: *write* and *read*. In school you learned to read and write. Now you are going to write and read. This is absolutely the key to using any daybook properly. For a few weeks you will have to make a real effort. You will have to keep reminding yourself to write and read, write and read. Soon it will become a habit. The basic principle is to write everything down and then remember to read it.

Many people think along these lines: "If I don't write it down, I might forget it. If I do write it down, I might forget to read it. I suppose I'd better just try to keep it in mind."

Well, it doesn't always work, as you know. We have all missed appointments, been late for a party, shown up without a covered dish, missed our parents' anniversary—not because we are inconsiderate or insensitive, but because there is just so much our minds can handle. And the more creative you are, the more ideas you will have swimming inside your head.

I remember two college fellows, roommates, who had decided to use an organizer to keep their lives under control. They were both very excited about the concept, and they were learning to write everything down, to plan their projects, to set their goals. They had been invited to dinner at a friend's house on a Friday night at 6:30. They both wrote the appointment in their books. Friday came. The week had been busy. They were thankful for the weekend and, without thinking, they just threw on their coats and headed for the cafeteria for dinner. They went through the line, got their heaping plates of spaghetti, and found a table where they could relax. As they were finishing their meal, one said to the other, "What time is it?" The answer was 6:35. When the time was mentioned, it was as if an alarm went off in their heads.

"Weren't we supposed to be somewhere at 6:30?" one said to the other. They grabbed their planners, which were right beside them, and read what they had written. They ran from the building, hopped in the car, raced to their friend's home, walked in apologizing for being late, and allowed themselves to be ushered to the dinner table for a home-cooked meal of spaghetti.

They had learned to write, but had failed to read. They were able to squeak by that one with only a stomach-ache. But not every situation can be handled quite that easily.

A CONSTANT COMPANION

Have you ever written a to-do list and forgotten to read it until it was too late? Have you ever written out an itinerary of errands that you had to run, stuck it in your pocket, and returned home and read it, only to find you had forgotten to make one stop? All of these things necessitate extra trips, extra phone calls, and extra work, which all translate into extra time.

In order to do things effectively, you must also learn to make your daybook your constant companion. Carry it everywhere. "Everywhere?" you ask. Yes, everywhere. Once in a while I will leave it in the car when I go to dinner with my husband or friends, but other than that it is with me all the time. Now, you may feel this is a little extreme, but I cannot begin to tell you how many minutes it saves me to always have it with me.

When people ask me if certain dates are open, I can answer them. I don't have to say, "I'll call you after I have checked my calendar." It saves me the time of a call, and the embarrassment of committing myself to something I cannot do. Whenever I have an idea, it gets written in the right place. When someone hands me a business card, a phone number, or the name of a person to contact, it's not stuffed in a pocket and lost in the next day's wash; it's stored in my daybook where I can easily retrieve it. If I have my planner with me, I always have my schedule, my plans, important telephone numbers, project information, ideas, special notes, my goals for reviewing regularly, and my to-do list at my fingertips. I don't waste any mental energy trying to remember details or appointments or things I was supposed to do while I was out.

I recall one young woman in one of my advanced seminars who was already using a daybook. She raised her hand one night.

"Donna, I have a baby now," she said. "I have to haul a diaper bag, purse, baby, and my planner. I don't think I can still carry my planner. Any suggestions?"

"Don't leave the baby home, for one thing," I said.

She laughed. "Right," she said. "That much I figured out on my own. And if I forget, my husband will be sure to remind me."

This time everyone laughed.

"Let me ask you this," I said. "Have you found your planner a help or a hindrance in your life as a new mother?"

"Couldn't exist without it," the woman testified. "When I'm waiting at the pediatrician's, I pull it out to review my questions for him. When I have to line up a babysitter, I tear out a sitter's memo page and leave all the needed information."

"Great!" I said. "You've just answered your own question. Since your planner is essential, you'll have to prioritize. Empty your purse of unneeded items and make room for your daybook. Carry fewer toys or disposable diapers in the diaper bag and make room for it. Just keep in mind the time, money, and energy you'll be saving by having your daybook handy. That motivation will make you creative enough to find a place for it."

The woman nodded and smiled. "You're right," she said. "I mean, if I could carry a ten-pound baby boy with me every moment for nine months, I ought to be able to carry a six-ounce planner, right?"

Again we all laughed.

Make your planner your constant companion. You might feel as though you're carrying an extra load for a while, but soon you will realize it is only an extra advantage.

WEAVING A TAPESTRY OF LIFE

In the next two chapters you will learn dozens of inside tips on how to use many forms to increase the efficiency of your life. Before beginning that, however, I would like you to once again take a few moments to consider your life as it now is and as you hope it will soon become.

For a minute, view your life as a tapestry. It is very long, with a border on the sides and at the top (boundaries to keep it from fraying). Imagine the various blends of color in your life tapestry. There is texture as well. The weave changes. There are smooth areas and spots where the threads are knotted and rough. The pattern changes. Sometimes the details are small and intricate; other places there are large splashes of shape and fine lines of distinction. And as you work toward the bottom of the tapestry, you notice that there is no border, only bare and loose threads. The tapestry is not complete, many hours of weaving remain.

Parts of your tapestry resemble the life tapestries of other women, for these are the common denominators of being women, household managers, wives, mothers, volunteer workers, employees. Similar colors, similar lines, similar texture would be evident if we laid them side-by-side. But no two tapestries are alike. They are valuable because they are unique. God created each of us individually. You are one of a kind, different from any other person in the world.

Each day you continue to create your tapestry. Someday that tapestry will end. The question is: Will it be complete? When the weaving stops, will you have accomplished your task? Consciously and unconsciously as you live you weave the threads of who you are, what you do, and what is important to you. You should be able to pick up your daybook and see your tapestry woven on its pages. Your personality, your interest, and your family should all be reflected in it.

Continue to weave those threads; keep on becoming who you want to be; complete your task. Be proud of your accomplishments. Someday your loved ones will look at that finished tapestry and say, "Look what she did with the time God gave her. She was an example of what can be accomplished in a lifetime."

TIME CHART

	Monday	Tuesday	Wednesday	Thursday	Friday	Saturday	Sunday
8:00							
8:30							
9:00							
9:30							
10:00							
10:30							
11:00							
11:30							
12:00							
12:30							
1:00							
1:30							
2:00							
2:30							
3:00							
3:30							
4:00							
4:30							
5:00							
5:30							

Form 2

ACTIVITIES EVALUATION

What I do currently			
Activity	**Actual Time Spent**	**Activity**	**Actual Time Spent**
Total:		**Total:**	

Grand Total: _____

What must I do? and *With time remaining, what do I want to do?*

Activity	**Time**	**Activity**	**Time**
Total:		**Total:**	

168 Hours Available

_____ **Hours Spent** _____ **Remaining Time Available**

Consider:

Amusement	Meal Preparation	Telephone
Civic Activities	(include eating)	Conversations
Church Activities	Planning	Thinking
Commuting	Prospecting	Waiting
Dressing & Clothes	Sleeping	Watching Television
Preparation	Studying	Working

5

Freedom in Forms, Forms, and More Forms

*H*ave you ever heard of Houdini?" I ask women in my seminars. Usually someone replies, "Oh, yes, he was a magician."

Houdini wasn't a magician. He was an escape artist.

Don't tell anyone, but I have discovered Houdini's secret. And I've been using it for 24 years.

Have you ever marveled at the way Houdini enjoyed being bound in chains and placed in a box, which was submerged under water? He thrived on the challenge of being bound. In fact, the more restrictions that were placed on him, the more creative he needed to become to free himself of his shackles.

In a sense we are all bound like Houdini. Every single one of us has things that bind us. Each of us is bound by a 24-hour day. Most of us are bound by our financial resources. Some of us have other limitations—emotional, physical, social, or spiritual.

Yet the key to our success, I believe, is the same as the key to Houdini's success. He allowed himself to be bound. He accepted, and even welcomed, limitations. With that attitude he was free to be creative and accomplish his goal within his framework. Often creativity doesn't start until we are limited.

Who is more creative, the woman who can go to the market and spend any amount of money on groceries or the woman who has a family of six to feed and can only spend $50 a week? Obviously the woman with less money. She is forced to learn how to exist on a limited budget. The old adage, "Necessity is the mother of invention," is true.

Houdini didn't just get locked up by chains and shackles and padlocks and thrown into a box, which was submerged under water, because someone forced him. He made a conscious choice to be an escape artist.

Igor Stravinsky, the famous composer, said in the *Poetics of Music*, "My freedom thus consists in my moving about within a narrow frame that I have assigned myself. ... My freedom will be so much the greater and more meaningful, the narrower I limit my field of action. ... Whatever diminishes constraint, diminishes strength. The more constraints one imposes, the more one frees oneself of the chains that shackle the spirit."

Is our spirit shackled because we have too much to do and not enough time to do it in or because we fight and kick at our limitations and wish we had a million dollars and eight maids to help us do our work? Or are we like Houdini, allowing ourselves to be freed by our limitations?

This is what a daybook does for us. We make the conscious choice to be bound to carrying a book, to writing in that book, to reading that book, to applying that book to the activities of our lives. As we do that, we find the freedom to be creative. That's what a daybook has done for me. That is what, I am sure, it will do for you.

If you already own a daybook set it next to you while you are reading this chapter and refer to it as I discuss each section. This chapter will teach you how to begin using your planner to its maximum potential. If you do not as yet own a daybook, overview the sample forms I've included. You can then create your own daybook from these forms.

Your daybook symbolizes a fresh start, a new opportunity to be consistent enough and disciplined enough to bring the bits and pieces of your life under control. It's fun to look at, so you almost hate to mark it up. But nothing will begin to happen until you begin to live with it and use it. Don't worry about how neat or pretty it remains.

At first glance your reaction might be, "There are too many forms. There's no way I'm going to use all of them." That's all right. Don't try to at first. When I first started using an organizer, I started with a calendar and "today" pages, plus one section marked "Misc." As the years progressed and I learned to make good use of the today pages, I began to realize the need for new forms and dividers. Don't be afraid to begin at that level. If you work with those calendars and today pages every day, you too will begin to expand your notebook. The advantages of additional sections and additional forms will become obvious.

Illustration 2

The prime prerequisite for a good organizer is that it be *expandable*. A daybook must be able to grow and change with you, since you are not the same person you were five years ago, and you will not be the same person next year. Your needs change. Your activities change. Your goals change. Your interests change. Your daybook should be of the loose-leaf variety, so you have the privilege of adding to it and changing the sections around to adapt to your present needs.

The next important thing to remember is that your daybook is *not* the place to store pieces of paper. It needs to be cleaned out and kept current. Everything in your planner should be something that you refer to or use at least monthly or for a designated time period. When you come to the end of the month, clean out the today pages. When you finish a project, take out your notes. When you wrap up your expenses for the month, move them. When you update your goals, replace the old ones. *But don't throw them away* (at least not everything).

Most of the forms in this book are valuable. The information becomes your tax records, your journal, your expense account, and your reference library. I suggest that you go to the drugstore and purchase several inexpensive cardboard loose-leaf binders of matching size and start your own storage system. Label the binders: Today Pages 1995, Goals, Expense Sheets, Women's Club, etc. When you move things from your planner, move them into the proper place in your storage binders. You will save time and effort by being able to retrieve names, telephone numbers, dates, and tax information at a moment's notice. It is pleasurable to go back and look at last year's goals and discover you have reached them. That gives you a source of motivation to keep moving toward future achievement.

THE NEED FOR STANDARDIZATION

When Henry Ford perfected the concept of making all automobile parts a standard size so that cars could be put together on assembly lines, he proved that standardization was a time and money saver. When all radiator caps and all door handles and all rear windows and all the other parts were identical in design, they could be rapidly and easily fitted onto a new or used car. Your daybook should also make use of the benefits of standardization. If your lifestyle is very active you may want a larger size daybook. Otherwise you might want to use a small size that will fit in your handbag or briefcase.

Material that is standardized is easier to hold, use, refer to, and file. Everything you insert into your planner ought to be on the same size of paper. Every portion you move out ought to go in storage notebooks of the same size. Keep a notepad that fits your book by the telephone, so you can record telephone numbers. Keep another notepad of the same size in the back of your book. Standardize everything. This makes organization easier.

I used to spend a great deal of time in stationery and card shops, selecting several packages of notepaper in a variety of designs. When I went to write a note, I would go through the long process of picking out just the right one for the right person. "Would Jane like the flowers or the cute little children better?" "Should I use formal or casual notepaper?" One day I realized how much time this was consuming, so I decided to save these valuable minutes. I had a friend design some notes for me, using my favorite flower. Then I had them printed in bulk. Now I use them for every note I write. I standardized this area of my life, and I have saved hours of time over the past few years.

I encourage you to think of areas of your life that can be standardized. Are you like some friends of mine who spend hours matching their kids' and husbands' socks? When Erma Bombeck's children and husband ask her, "Where is the matching sock?" she replies, "What do you mean, 'Where is the matching sock?' Speak to the sock-eating washing machine."

Why not buy your husband the same dark socks? Couldn't the kids wear white socks at least 50 percent of the time?

We'll talk more about standardizing other areas of your life in later chapters.

Standardization will streamline many of your daily activities so you can use that time for something more productive and far more creative.

WHAT TO LOOK FOR

Your planner is a tool of organization, powered by your desire to bring order into your life, activated by your mental stimulation, propelled by your personal and consistent use. *Personal* organization is controlled "individuality." Therefore, you will want to begin with a binder that is very durable so it can go everywhere with you. The covers of some binders overlap and close with a Velcro fastener so that the edges of your papers won't fray and so that things can't fall out. But any sturdy leather or vinyl standard binder will do.

Somewhere in your binder, there should be holders for your pen and pencil. (If you are using a 3-ring binder, a plastic, zippered pouch works well.) You will always need a pencil. Perhaps you will even eventually use colored pencils. A pen is important, but not for writing on the calendar and today pages. Write in pencil. Your planner will be less cluttered. Discipline yourself to put the pen and pencil back where they belong; then you will not have to dig into the bottom of your purse to find something to write with. You will not make someone wait on the telephone or in the school lobby while you try to borrow a pen from a passerby.

At the front of your daybook, place a plastic, see-through zippered pouch, available anywhere organizers are sold. Use it to store your scissors, rubber bands, paper clips, postage stamps, name tags, Band-Aids, ink pen refills, coins for the parking meter or telephone or Laundromat, claim checks from the cleaners, parking stubs, a ruler, or your favorite family snapshots. This bag will hold all the unwieldy items that are so essential. One woman I know has four zippered bags in her planner, each under a different section.

You might also want to invest in a page of transparent pockets, the kind that are just the right size for a foil packet of Alka-Seltzer, a book of stamps, school pictures of the children, your library card, all credit cards, packets of sugar substitute, business cards, or your contact lens flat-case.

If your daybook does become your mind, as mine is, you will not want to lose it. I have typed a small notice, "If found, please return. Reward offered," which I taped to the front page of my planner. My "mind" is worth $10 or $20 for sure.

BASIC FORMS

The first form in your planner should list your personal information. (See Form 4 at the end of this chapter.) Since some planners serve as a substitute for your purse or wallet, it is important to have the same sort of emergency data listed in it as you would your wallet. Besides, if your planner should ever get misplaced, you will want someone to be able to return it to you. Also, because this page will be turned a lot, it's good to have it printed on light card stock.

As you build your daybook, you may want to add divider pages that group related forms into convenient sections. For example, you may want to have a divider for calendar pages, for meals, for goals, etc. These can be made of light card stock, available at stationery stores or print shops. Attach a colored tab divider and you're all set to arrange your planner in a way that's most useful to you.

Three-Year Calendar

The next form is the three-year calendar (Form 5 at the end of this chapter). You can photocopy the calendar on your check register for this purpose. Use this calendar to plan holidays and long-term vacation arrangements, to schedule business conventions, and to set the dates for your one-year, two-year, and three-year goals. When Anissa was young, she and I would spend a few days at a place called Pinetop during the second week of July with a friend of mine and her children. We would block out the dates a couple of years in advance, since these days are important to us. You may want to use this calendar to mark the dates of a family reunion, or your husband's vacation, which probably falls in the same time frame each year.

Special Occasions Page

Record birthdays, anniversaries, and other major events that need to be remembered annually on the special occasions page (Form 6), which you can copy onto the reverse side of the three-year calendar. If you are like me and come from a big family with lots of relatives, this space may not be ample. I record special dates on January through December dividers with tabs. I guarantee that this little piece of paper will save you a lot of embarrassment, last-minute phone calls, trips to the post office, and money usually spent on greeting cards that begin with the awkward phrase, "I'm sorry I missed your..."

At the beginning of each month, you may prefer to transfer that month's special occasions to your monthly calendar and the today pages, which we will look at shortly. Remember to put a reminder on a preceding date far enough ahead to allow you time to purchase a gift or mail a card. Another way of doing this is to develop a reminder system. Put a yellow dot beside the date on the today page or monthly calendar, and remember that the yellow dot means a special occasion. You then can check back to the page where they are listed. When you learn to use this system well, Aunt Sara will say, "It's so nice to be remembered on my eightieth birthday!"

Monthly Calendar Page

Monthly calendar pages let you see your month at a glance. These are sometimes easier to purchase than to make. Either way, obtain pages for each of the next 18 months (Form 7). Sometimes women wonder, "Why do I need these monthly pages when there are also individual day pages?"

"To plan your month in advance," I always answer. "A quick look at the two pages for each month, and you can tell if you're going to be pressed for time that month. As I've said before, you can say no to some invitation or duty because you know the month is already crowded."

Remember to write on these pages and the today pages with pencil only. If you don't and your life is anything like mine, you will end up with items scratched out, which makes the pages hard to read, and leaves very little space for new notations.

The monthly pages are not for detail, but for major events only. Write a few words, or even single words, but not details. Block out segments of time: home days, appointments, trips, and monthly activities. Be conscious of preparation time, which needs to be scheduled in most cases. Remember, if you don't plan your time, someone else will. When someone asks if you can commit yourself to a project or a dinner engagement, you will be able to look not only at the specific date, but also at the schedule that surrounds that date, which will prevent you from overloading some weeks. If you work as an independent manager or you find one month of the year busier than others, this habit of reviewing the date (as well as the day prior and the day following) will keep you on target.

You may want to establish a color system that can be used throughout your book. Use a different color pencil to symbolize each child. This way you will know which child you are carpooling and which child has a dental appointment. Another option is to use different color pencils for various consistent activities in your life. If you are an avid tennis player and are involved in many related activities, write everything that has anything to do with tennis in one color pencil, social commitments in another, and all church activities in a third color.

Having these monthly calendars at your fingertips will save you time in long-term planning and scheduling. Suppose, for example, you have a dentist appointment, and as you leave, the dentist tells you to return in six months. You get to the desk in the outer office and the nurse asks if you wish to go ahead and schedule the appointment at that time. If you do, she writes it on a little card, but you run the risk of losing the card or of finding out you didn't remember that you would be on vacation at that particular time. If you tell her you will schedule the appointment later, you either forget about it or waste the time making an additional call.

When you have your planner with you, you can simply make the appointment, write it down in the right place in the right month, and put it out of your mind. At the end of my monthly calendar section, I keep a blank sheet to add any dates beyond that time period. Then I transfer these dates to my new month-at-a-glance pages when I add them. Make tab dividers for each month: January, February, March, etc.

DAY-TO-DAY OPERATIONS

The planner section or today pages of your daybook will become the main focus for your daily organization. (See Form 8, end of chapter.) This is where you will *write* and *read* with more regularity than anywhere else. These are the pages that will become today's action and tomorrow's memories. Often when I am waiting, relaxing, or planning, I look at the next few days' activities. Reviewing these pages at the end of each day tells me exactly what is in store for tomorrow and how I need to prepare. Can I sleep a little later or do I need to get up a few minutes earlier?

A number of years ago when we were expecting 15 guests for Thanksgiving, my husband found me in my study writing a letter at 11:00 A.M. He poked his head in and asked, "What? No Thanksgiving dinner panic? No last-minute jitters? No chaos, no pandemonium?" I shook my head and answered in mock smugness, "Who *me*, panic? Never! Actually, it's rather boring being prepared so far in advance and having to wait for everyone to arrive." We laughed together. We both could recall some earlier years in our marriage when planning a large dinner had sent me and the entire household into an uproar. But not anymore. Not since I developed my daybook.

Thanks to my preprinted shopping lists, I no longer had to scramble to the grocery store at the last minute for some forgotten items. My household chore list had enabled me to get the house so clean, I no longer found myself standing on a chair trying to dust a dirty dining room chandelier after the table was already set. My menu planner solved the problem of trying to use ice cubes to get Jell-O to set as the guests were walking in the front door. Believe me, there were many holidays when all these, and many other last-minute details had caused me to be a basket case. But now, my daybook helps take the panic out of holidays.

Today Page

You may experiment with two or three months, but I suggest that you keep at least one month of dated today pages in your daybook at all times. When you end the month, store the pages if the information is necessary for future use or preparation, and put in a new month. Keep your planner current.

Start by dating each page. I recommend you date at least two weeks of each month in advance. Circle the day of the week and write in the month and the date.

The nice thing about having unprinted pages is the flexibility. If you really mess up, replace the page. If you have a day that is particularly full of details, a special occasion for example, you may want to use two pages. Again, use it to fit your lifestyle and your individual needs. A today page is nothing more than a glorified to-do list (see Form 8). When I'm on vacation, I divide the day pages in half, so one page can be used for two days. After all, my vacation days are not filled with appointments and commitments, or at least they shouldn't be.

On the lefthand side of the page, space is provided to write your appointments: "Hair appointment at 9:30; School conference at 11:00; Committee meeting at 1:30; Carpool at 3:45." Women who work outside of the home can use the space to record staff meetings, sales interviews, luncheon appointments, or business conferences. At the top of the righthand side is your to-do list. There is a spot for the main event of your day, the number-one priority task that absolutely must be accomplished. The rest of the list can be labeled A, B, or C priority; or 1, 2, 3, or color-coded (red for urgent jobs) if you find that easier. I find that a rating system often motivates me to complete the entire list. Items that do not get done can be moved to the next day's to-do list. Or make a note to yourself on the next day's sheet to check the previous day's list. When you do transfer them, you may choose to give these items a higher rating so that they don't keep reappearing day after day.

The "To-Buy" box is *not* the spot for your grocery list. There is a special section for that. This area is for the things that need to be bought in special places or errands that need to be run throughout the day. For example, if I am meeting a friend for lunch at a restaurant in a particular shopping center, I might be able to purchase my hose from my favorite department store at the same time and save myself from making a special trip. If my husband is working on a special yard project and he needs me to buy a certain piece of equipment, this is where I would list it. An eyelash curler, a special kind of makeup, or shoes for your son are all things that need to be purchased in the least amount of time. By writing these items down (and always having my book with me), I am able to make purchases whenever I am near those stores.

The section marked "To Call" is to remind you of calls that need to be made and to help organize your telephoning so that you can do most of it in one block of time. Try to write the numbers beside the names so you will not have to waste time looking them up. Check off the calls as you complete them. If you are unable to reach someone, don't forget to move that name to the next day, or to make the necessary entry. Sometimes I just go back and check four or five days to see if there are names that haven't been crossed off.

The note section of the page can be used for whatever you want. Perhaps you will use it to write just a couple of lines at the end of each day as a daily journal. Maybe you will use it for a few notes from a very important meeting, details of a scheduled doctor's appointment, or as a tally of daily expenses. This is a good place to keep track of mileage if you need a record for business.

If you are a working woman, the today pages combine your personal and business life. Keep your book with you on your desk at work. When the kids check in by phone in the afternoon and inform you of a soccer game next Tuesday, write it down. When you are at work and remember things you should have done at home, write them down, and vice versa. The today pages will replace that awful gnawing question, "Have I forgotten something?" with the positive assurance, "Everything is under control."

Menu Planner

Each day, the three o'clock doldrums usually are initiated when you begin to wonder, *What am I going to fix for supper?* It is such a hassle to come up with new and interesting ideas at the last minute. If you learn to use the menu planner (Form 9), you will find release from the pressure of this daily dilemma and erase that weary question from your mind.

The menu planner is designed to outline your menu plans for two or all three meals per day for an entire week in advance. Once you are in the swing of this, you will be able to plan a week in advance in 15 minutes, which will save you anywhere from 30 minutes to two hours a week. Most women have no idea how much time they waste staring at cupboard shelves hoping desperately for an idea, making last-minute trips to the grocery store to get extra food for one meal, and flipping through recipe books trying to figure out what to do with the only thing left in the freezer. The menu planner will give you back that time, *and* give you back some pocket money. It logically dovetails into your grocery list, eliminating the guesswork. If you glance at your coming week's schedule while you're planning your meals, you will know which night to have the meal that takes the most or least preparation time.

Hanging the menus on a refrigerator door where everyone can see them is of benefit to you. If you are running late, there is no reason why other family members can't get supper started. You won't have to rush in out of breath and hear, "We would have started something for dinner but we didn't know what you were going to fix."

Be sure to date and fill in your menu planner with pencil so that you can erase the dates a month or a year later and simply rerun the same week of menus. This will save you a 15- to 30-minute planning session.

Shopping Checklist

Having planned your menus for the week, the next logical step is to prepare a shopping list of the items you will need in order to fix the food for each meal. Here again, your daybook can be set up to serve your needs, this time with printed shopping checklists (Form 10). Notice that most of the work has been done for you, since the items that most of us purchase regularly are already printed on the pages. They are divided into categories the same way you will find them at the grocery store. All you have to do is list the quantity desired. Every time you think of anything that is needed for your home or family, check it off. If you can't find the item on the list, there is an entire section for you to write in the additional purchases as well as blanks in each category. There is a column for you to write in the price of the item and space available to add up what you are spending. This information can be transferred to the household budget section, which we will examine later, and it will help you realize how much you are spending as you purchase each item. Note also the column to check if you have a money-saving coupon for that item or purchases from stores that are having special sales.

Your grocery list reflects your social life. If you have been asked to take a green-bean casserole to the potluck dinner, write down the date and, as quickly as possible, add the items you need for the casserole to your grocery list. Just remember, never question that list. I have been at the market and looked at my grocery list and wondered, "What do I need the green beans for?"

Not knowing the answer, I don't buy them. Once I'm home, I remember the green beans are for my friend's potluck dinner on Saturday. Take it from me: Always buy what is on your list. You'll never regret it.

Have you ever run to the store for one item and returned with four bags jammed full of groceries? You are putting the last few items away when your son walks into the kitchen and says, "Oh, good, you've been to the store. Now I can finish my school project. Where's the glue you bought me?" The glue is the item you went to purchase. Instead, you have a receipt for $67.92 of groceries. Surely you could remember *one thing* during the time it took you to drive from the house to the grocery store. But you couldn't. Because the school project is due at 8:30 the next morning, you make another trip. And every trip to the market lightens your purse an average of $9. *Write and read.* Don't head for the store without a prepared list and your daybook. By using a well-prepared, organized grocery list, you will buy fewer impulse items and your shopping will be easier, more economical, and indeed, time saving. For every minute you spend in the market over 30 minutes, you will spend $2.50.

Children and husband tend to buy larger sizes of everything than we weekly shoppers do. If you want to avoid boxes that don't fit on your shelves, quantities you will never use, and brands you have never heard of, send a *detailed* grocery list along with a less experienced shopper.

The grocery list section of your daybook will become a practical and dependable part of your weekly planning schedule. By having it with you at all times, you will be able to stop at the store on the way home or in between appointments without the frustration of knowing that your list is back home on the kitchen counter. Use these forms. They work.

Fast-Food Calorie Counter

It's probably not fair to go from the grocery section to the diet section, but one should influence the other. Most women today are concerned about their eating habits and those of their families. If you don't use this section to help you keep your weight control program on target, you can adapt it to keep track of your health maintenance program.

If you have at least one child in your home, you have probably come face to face with every type of hamburger and french fry known to man. If you have teenagers, you have lived for many years in a world that smells of tacos and pepperoni pizzas. The calorie counter (Form 11) will let you know exactly how much damage you're doing the next time you attack a chocolate shake or a bean burrito. Watch out for Wendy's "triple with cheese." Remember, food is just fuel to do the work!

Calorie and Carbohydrate Guide

Another valuable form is the calorie and carbohydrate guide (Form 12) for many of the basic foods that appear frequently in our daily diets. This little page, front and back, can help you stay within your limits and keep you in shape. The calorie burn-off guide will tell you exactly how far you have to run to wear off the effects of the spaghetti and garlic bread you ate at supper!

Diet Form

The diet form (Form 13) itself gives you space to write down what you have eaten and how many calories you have consumed. There is enough space for a whole week's records on one sheet.

Fitness Program Form

Record your planned exercise or fitness program each day of the week on this page (Form 14). You may even record your hours of sleep, your weight (both morning and evening), and whether or not you took your vitamins for the day. Remember, the best sleeping hours occur before midnight!

I loathe exercise, as I mentioned before. I never had to bother with walking or jogging or doing situps, since I weighed 103 pounds until I was 30 years old. Then all of a sudden I began to gain a pound a month. After 19 months, my husband asked, "Is this a trend? If so, when does it end?"

I didn't answer him. I allowed another ten months to roll by and another ten pounds to roll on, until even I realized I had a problem. Then I started to exercise. Guess what? I felt better and had more energy. I even lost ten pounds.

This fitness program is a new one for me. It "jogs" my memory and encourages me to keep on trying. Disciplining myself to stick with a regular program is difficult; I've tried everything at least once and failed. My organizer and "advance decision-making" practice have helped me stick to a regular exercise program. I hope your daybook does the same. Exercise not only keeps your body in shape, it also builds your stamina so that you can do *all* God plans for you.

Babysitter Memos

Babysitter memos (Form 15) are designed to be time savers. Leave this filled-out form with your sitter when you go out, and she will have all the necessary information to do her job correctly and to reach you in case of an emergency. Similarly, if you have any calls or visitors while you're out, she can record the information on the same form. This protects the sitter, your children, and you. If you no longer need babysitters, allow your teenager to take this list when he or she babysits. Such organization made my daughter a very popular sitter.

Housecleaning List

The housecleaning list (Form 16) provides you with another organizational tool. The items are listed by rooms, with regular chores recorded first and a few lines for you to add special things that need to be accomplished in any particular room. Just check the completed column when you have finished the task.

Every home is different; every housekeeper is different. Therefore, there is a section at the bottom of the housecleaning list for chores that are not listed but need to be done at *your* house. I've laughingly told women that my mother washes the top of her refrigerator daily. It's true! But I have also reassured them that I have not carried on this family tradition. There will always be things that I will do in my cleaning that you will do another way. We all develop our own systems. The point is, the cleaning needs to be done regularly. Being proud of your home, allowing yourself the privilege of enjoying friends, and the warmth of hospitality are the rewards of being organized and orderly.

When I'm on a plane coming home from a speaking engagement, I think of 93 projects that need to be done at home. Housework seems so easy when you are sitting in an airplane rather than in the midst of a cluttered house. This housecleaning list helps to channel my enthusiasm so I am more realistic about the prospect of cleaning the bath, which includes scrubbing the sink, the tub, the commode, and the floor. The list also helps me organize my housework while I have some uninterrupted moments of peace.

You can also use this form for your children when they help around the house. Tell them to check off the items as they finish them. You will probably need to make a final inspection, but you will find better results when children know exactly what they are supposed to work on. You can't expect what you don't inspect.

Note the household cleaning supplies you are running low on in the grocery section of your shopping checklist. This will save you the frustration of not having what you need the next time you clean.

FREE TO BE YOU!

This chapter began with Houdini's secret: He allowed himself to be bound. Can you see how your planner gives you the same freedom to work within your own individual limitations? Beginning with those five denominators most women have in common, each of us is free to be versatile within a wide variety of activities.

Houdini didn't just say "Abracadabra" and have the chains fall off. He had a system. Lock by lock, chain by chain, he systematically freed himself. He planned and prepared for each event by the food he ate, the clothes he wore, even by the equipment he used. He had a plan. He didn't just get into that box, allow it to be lowered to the ocean floor, and then say to himself, "Which chain shall I try to unlock first?" He knew he first had to get those chains off his wrist so his hands were free to work. He had learned how to use his legs and feet to rid himself of those chains at the same time he was working on the chains around his neck and shoulders with his hands. He had prepared and he had planned and he had allowed himself to be bound Then his creative juices were free to flow.

In the same way, we have the equipment and the tools to become productive and free. Isn't it exciting? But remember our freedom starts from within. It starts with an attitude. Like Houdini, we must first allow ourselves to be bound to this tool, a daybook. Then you will be set free from the pressure of time.

I have been using a daybook for 24 years and my personal one is quite fat. Over the years it has grown along with me. (You can read into that whatever you please.) The more I use it, the more uses I find for it.

In this chapter we have examined the basic hands-on functions of a daybook. You now know ways in which it can help you organize your meals, shopping, cleaning, yearly schedules, and daily activities. Keep in mind that you can adapt any planner you own with these forms to make it work for *you!* Keep growing!

In our next chapter we will discover ways in which your planner can help you enhance your personal development, your people skills, and your life goals and career objectives

PERSONAL INFORMATION

Name _____

Address _____

_____ Phone _____

Business Address _____

_____ Phone _____

Driving Information _____

Lic Plate # _____

Registration # _____

Drivers lic. # _____

Auto Ins Co _____

Ins. Agent _____

Phone _____

Emergency Information _____

Health Ins. Co. _____

Policy # _____

Homeowners Ins. Co _____

Policy # _____

Agent _____

Phone _____

Notify in Case of Emergency _____

Name _____

Address _____

Phone _____

Form 4

1995

January
S	M	T	W	T	F	S
1	2	3	4	5	6	7
8	9	10	11	12	13	14
15	16	17	18	19	20	21
22	23	24	25	26	27	28
29	30	31				

February
S	M	T	W	T	F	S
			1	2	3	4
5	6	7	8	9	10	11
12	13	14	15	16	17	18
19	20	21	22	23	24	25
26	27	28				

March
S	M	T	W	T	F	S
			1	2	3	4
5	6	7	8	9	10	11
12	13	14	15	16	17	18
19	20	21	22	23	24	25
26	27	28	29	30	31	

April
S	M	T	W	T	F	S
						1
2	3	4	5	6	7	8
9	10	11	12	13	14	15
16	17	18	19	20	21	22
23/30	24	25	26	27	28	29

May
S	M	T	W	T	F	S
	1	2	3	4	5	6
7	8	9	10	11	12	13
14	15	16	17	18	19	20
21	22	23	24	25	26	27
28	29	30	31			

June
S	M	T	W	T	F	S
				1	2	3
4	5	6	7	8	9	10
11	12	13	14	15	16	17
18	19	20	21	22	23	24
25	26	27	28	29	30	

July
S	M	T	W	T	F	S
						1
2	3	4	5	6	7	8
9	10	11	12	13	14	15
16	17	18	19	20	21	22
23/30	24/31	25	26	27	28	29

August
S	M	T	W	T	F	S
		1	2	3	4	5
6	7	8	9	10	11	12
13	14	15	16	17	18	19
20	21	22	23	24	25	26
27	28	29	30	31		

September
S	M	T	W	T	F	S
					1	2
3	4	5	6	7	8	9
10	11	12	13	14	15	16
17	18	19	20	21	22	23
24	25	26	27	28	29	30

October
S	M	T	W	T	F	S
1	2	3	4	5	6	7
8	9	10	11	12	13	14
15	16	17	18	19	20	21
22	23	24	25	26	27	28
29	30	31				

November
S	M	T	W	T	F	S
			1	2	3	4
5	6	7	8	9	10	11
12	13	14	15	16	17	18
19	20	21	22	23	24	25
26	27	28	29	30		

December
S	M	T	W	T	F	S
					1	2
3	4	5	6	7	8	9
10	11	12	13	14	15	16
17	18	19	20	21	22	23
24/31	25	26	27	28	29	30

1996

January
S	M	T	W	T	F	S
	1	2	3	4	5	6
7	8	9	10	11	12	13
14	15	16	17	18	19	20
21	22	23	24	25	26	27
28	29	30	31			

February
S	M	T	W	T	F	S
				1	2	3
4	5	6	7	8	9	10
11	12	13	14	15	16	17
18	19	20	21	22	23	24
25	26	27	28	29		

March
S	M	T	W	T	F	S
					1	2
3	4	5	6	7	8	9
10	11	12	13	14	15	16
17	18	19	20	21	22	23
24/31	25	26	27	28	29	30

April
S	M	T	W	T	F	S
	1	2	3	4	5	6
7	8	9	10	11	12	13
14	15	16	17	18	19	20
21	22	23	24	25	26	27
28	29	30				

May
S	M	T	W	T	F	S
			1	2	3	4
5	6	7	8	9	10	11
12	13	14	15	16	17	18
19	20	21	22	23	24	25
26	27	28	29	30	31	

June
S	M	T	W	T	F	S
						1
2	3	4	5	6	7	8
9	10	11	12	13	14	15
16	17	18	19	20	21	22
23/30	24	25	26	27	28	29

July
S	M	T	W	T	F	S
	1	2	3	4	5	6
7	8	9	10	11	12	13
14	15	16	17	18	19	20
21	22	23	24	25	26	27
28	29	30	31			

August
S	M	T	W	T	F	S
				1	2	3
4	5	6	7	8	9	10
11	12	13	14	15	16	17
18	19	20	21	22	23	24
25	26	27	28	29	30	31

September
S	M	T	W	T	F	S
1	2	3	4	5	6	7
8	9	10	11	12	13	14
15	16	17	18	19	20	21
22	23	24	25	26	27	28
29	30					

October
S	M	T	W	T	F	S
		1	2	3	4	5
6	7	8	9	10	11	12
13	14	15	16	17	18	19
20	21	22	23	24	25	26
27	28	29	30	31		

November
S	M	T	W	T	F	S
					1	2
3	4	5	6	7	8	9
10	11	12	13	14	15	16
17	18	19	20	21	22	23
24	25	26	27	28	29	30

December
S	M	T	W	T	F	S
1	2	3	4	5	6	7
8	9	10	11	12	13	14
15	16	17	18	19	20	21
22	23	24	25	26	27	28
29	30	31				

1997

January
S	M	T	W	T	F	S
			1	2	3	4
5	6	7	8	9	10	11
12	13	14	15	16	17	18
19	20	21	22	23	24	25
26	27	28	29	30	31	

February
S	M	T	W	T	F	S
						1
2	3	4	5	6	7	8
9	10	11	12	13	14	15
16	17	18	19	20	21	22
23	24	25	26	27	28	

March
S	M	T	W	T	F	S
						1
2	3	4	5	6	7	8
9	10	11	12	13	14	15
16	17	18	19	20	21	22
23	24	25	26	27	28	29
30	31					

April
S	M	T	W	T	F	S
		1	2	3	4	5
6	7	8	9	10	11	12
13	14	15	16	17	18	19
20	21	22	23	24	25	26
27	28	29	30			

May
S	M	T	W	T	F	S
				1	2	3
4	5	6	7	8	9	10
11	12	13	14	15	16	17
18	19	20	21	22	23	24
25	26	27	28	29	30	31

June
S	M	T	W	T	F	S
1	2	3	4	5	6	7
8	9	10	11	12	13	14
15	16	17	18	19	20	21
22	23	24	25	26	27	28
29	30					

July
S	M	T	W	T	F	S
		1	2	3	4	5
6	7	8	9	10	11	12
13	14	15	16	17	18	19
20	21	22	23	24	25	26
27	28	29	30	31		

August
S	M	T	W	T	F	S
					1	2
3	4	5	6	7	8	9
10	11	12	13	14	15	16
17	18	19	20	21	22	23
24/31	25	26	27	28	29	30

September
S	M	T	W	T	F	S
	1	2	3	4	5	6
7	8	9	10	11	12	13
14	15	16	17	18	19	20
21	22	23	24	25	26	27
28	29	30				

October
S	M	T	W	T	F	S
			1	2	3	4
5	6	7	8	9	10	11
12	13	14	15	16	17	18
19	20	21	22	23	24	25
26	27	28	29	30	31	

November
S	M	T	W	T	F	S
						1
2	3	4	5	6	7	8
9	10	11	12	13	14	15
16	17	18	19	20	21	22
23	24	25	26	27	28	29
30						

December
S	M	T	W	T	F	S
	1	2	3	4	5	6
7	8	9	10	11	12	13
14	15	16	17	18	19	20
21	22	23	24	25	26	27
28	29	30	31			

SPECIAL OCCASIONS PAGE

JAN	JUL
FEB	AUG
MAR	SEP
APR	OCT
MAY	NOV
JUN	DEC

MONTHLY CALENDAR PAGE

Month: _____   Year: _____

Monday	Tuesday	Wednesday

Thursday	Friday	Saturday/Sunday

TODAY PAGE

Today

SUN   MON   TUE   WED   THU   FRI   SAT

Date

APPOINTMENTS	TO DO	ABC ✔	
A.M. 7	#1 Priority		
8			
9			
10			
11			
P.M. 12	To Buy		
1			
2	To Call Phone No.		
3			
4			
5			
6	Mileage		
7	Ending		
	Beginning		
	Total		

NOTE:

Item Expense   **Amount**

Form 8

MENU PLANNER

Week of

	BREAKFAST	LUNCH	DINNER
S U N			
M O N			
T U E			
W E D			
T H U			
F R I			
S A T			

Form 9

SHOPPING CHECKLIST

	Qty	Cost	Coup		Qty	Cost	Coup		Qty	Cost	Coup
FROZEN FOOD/JUICE				**STAPLES**				Buns	—	——	—
Ice Cream	—	——	—	Flour	—	——	—		—	——	—
				Sugar	—	——	—		—	——	—
Vegetables	—	——	—	Cereal	—	——	—		—	——	—
	—	——	—		—	——	—	**PAPER GOODS**			
	—	——	—		—	——	—	Paper			
	—	——	—	Mixes	—	——	—	Towels	—	——	—
	—	——	—	Nuts	—	——	—	Tissue			
	—	——	—	Jello	—	——	—	(facial)	—	——	—
Prepared				**SPICES**				Toilet Paper	—	——	—
Dinners				Bacon Bits	—	——	—	Napkins	—	——	—
	—	——	—	Coconut				Plastic			
Juice	—	——	—	Chocolate	—	——	—	Wrap	—	——	—
	—	——	—	Baking				Waxed			
				Soda	—	——	—	Paper	—	——	—
CONDIMENTS				Baking				Foil	—	——	—
Syrup	—	——	—	Powder	—	——	—	Trash Bags	—	——	—
Molasses	—	——	—	Salt/Pepper	—	——	—	Zip Bags:			
Jelly/Jam	—	——	—		—	——	—	Small	—	——	—
Peanut					—	——	—	Large	—	——	—
Butter	—	——	—		—	——	—	**HOUSEHOLD**			
Honey	—	——	—		—	——	—	Dishwasher			
Shortening	—	——	—	**PASTA**				Soap	—	——	—
Oil	—	——	—	Spaghetti	—	——	—	Dish Soap	—	——	—
Catsup	—	——	—	Pasta	—	——	—	Clothes Soap	—	——	—
Mustard	—	——	—	Rice	—	——	—	Bleach			
Vinegar	—	——	—	Instant				White	—	——	—
Mayonnaise	—	——	—	Potatoes	—	——	—	Colors	—	——	—
Pickles	—	——	—	Mixes	—	——	—	Fabric			
Relish	—	——	—		—	——	—	Softener	—	——	—
Salad	—	——	—		—	——	—	Furniture			
Dressing					—	——	—	Polish	—	——	—
Croutons	—	——	—	**DRINKS**				Light Bulbs	—	——	—
CANNED GOODS				Coffee	—	——	—	Vacuum Bags	—	——	—
Soups	—	——	—	Tea	—	——	—	Pet Food	—	——	—
	—	——	—	Juice	—	——	—		—	——	—
Canned					—	——	—		—	——	—
Meat	—	——	—	Sparkling	—	——	—		—	——	—
Tuna	—	——	—	Colas	—	——	—		—	——	—
Canned					—	——	—		—	——	—
Meals	—	——	—		—	——	—	**MEAT**			
CANNED VEGETABLES					—	——	—	Beef	—	——	—
Tomato Sauce/					—	——	—		—	——	—
Paste	—	——	—	**PASTRY**				Chicken	—	——	—
Vegetables	—	——	—	Crackers	—	——	—		—	——	—
	—	——	—	Cookies	—	——	—		—	——	—
	—	——	—	Chips	—	——	—		—	——	—
	—	——	—	Breads	—	——	—		—	——	—
	—	——	—		—	——	—		—	——	—
	—	——	—		—	——	—		—	——	—
	—	——	—		—	——	—		—	——	—
	—	——	—		—	——	—		—	——	—

	Qty	Cost	Coup		Qty	Cost	Coup		Qty	Cost	Coup
DAIRY				Cheese:							
Milk				Yellow							
Butter											
Cheese											
				White				Toothpaste			
Eggs								Deodorant			
Cottage								Hair Care			
Cheese				Prepared							
Sour Cream				Salad				Hand Soap			
Yogurt								Body Soap			
								Facial			
								Cleanser			
FRESH PRODUCE								Feminine			
Vegetables								Protection			
								Razors			
				BAKERY				Shaving			
Fruit				Sweet Rolls				Cream			
				Cake							
				Doughnuts							
				Pie							
				Cookies							
INTERNATIONAL FOODS											
Chinese											
				SCHOOL & OFFICE							
				Pens							
				Pencils							
Mexican				Paper							
				Notebooks							
				3 x 5 Cards							
Italian											
DELI											
Sliced Meat											
				PERSONAL ITEMS							
				Makeup							

FAST-FOOD CALORIE COUNT

Items	Cal	Fat	Items	Cal	Fat
Kentucky Fried Chicken			**Burger King®**		
Original Recipe Chicken			Hamburger	260	10
Wing	150	8	with cheese	300	14
Drumstick	130	7	Whopper	630	39
Breast	360	20	with cheese	720	46
Thigh	260	17	Double Whopper		
Extra Crispy Chicken			with cheese	950	63
Wing	200	13	Applie Pie	310	15
Drumstick	190	11	Onion Rings	310	14
Breast	470	28	French Fries	400	20
Thigh	370	25	Chocolate Shake	310	7
McDonald's			Vanilla Shake	310	7
Egg McMuffin	200	11	**Wendy's Old-Fashioned**		
Hot cakes with butter			**Hamburgers**		
and syrup	435	12	Hamburger (single)	350	15
Scrambled eggs (2)	140	10	Jr. Burger	270	9
Hash browns	130	7	Burger with everything	440	23
Pork sausage	160	15	Chili	190	6
English Muffin			French Fries	340	17
with butter	170	4	Frosty	340	10
Hamburger	255	9	**Arby's®**		
Cheeseburger	305	13	Roast Beef	383	18.2
Quarter Pounder	410	20	Beef 'n' Cheese	508	26.5
with Cheese	510	28	Super Roast Beef	552	28.3
Big Mac	500	26	Junior Roast Beef	233	10.8
French Fries (M)	320	17	Ham 'n' Cheese	355	14.2
Jack in the Box			Turkey Sub	486	19
Hamburger	280	11	Lite	260	6
Cheeseburger	330	15	French Fries	246	13
Jumbo Jack®	560	32	Apple Turnover	303	18.3
with Cheese	610	36	**Taco Bell**		
Regular Taco	190	11	Taco	183	11
Super Taco	280	17	Nachos	346	18
Fish Supreme	590	32	Pintos 'n' Cheese	190	9
Country Fried Steak	450	25	Tostada	243	11
Breakfast Jack®	300	12	Bean Burrito	381	14
French Fries (reg)	350	17	Burrito Supreme	440	22
Onion Rings	380	23			
Apple Turnover	350	19			

CALORIE AND CARBOHYDRATE GUIDE

Food	Size	Cal	Carb	Food	Size	Cal	Carb
Cereals				Potato chips	10 med.	115	10
Bran flakes	1 cup	105	28	Potato, French fried	10 pcs.	155	20
Corn flakes	1 cup	121	21	Sauerkraut	1/2 cup	20	3
Corn grits	1/2 cup	60	13	Spinach, boiled	1/2 cup	20	3
Cooked wheat	1/2 cup	55	11	Squash, summer	1/2 cup	15	4
Oatmeal	1/2 cup	65	11	Sweet potato	1 med.	155	36
Bread and Pastries				Tomato	1 med.	30	6
Biscuits, baking powder	1	105	13	Turnips	1/2 cup	18	4
Bread, French	2 slices	146	26	**Beef, Lamb, Pork**			
Bread, raisin	2 slices	150	26	Bacon strips	2 avg.	90	1
Bread, rye	2 slices	120	26	Beef heart	3 oz.	160	1
Bread, white	2 slices	140	26	Beef liver	3 oz.	195	1
Bread, whole wheat	2 slices	120	24	Beef roast (incl. fat)	3 oz.	375	0
Buns, hot dog/hamburger	1	120	21	Beef steak (incl. fat)	3 oz.	330	0
Crackers, graham	1 (4"-sq.)	110	25	Beef tongue	3 oz.	205	trace
Crackers, rye	1	23	5	Bologna	1 slice	40	trace
Crackers, soda	1 (4"-sq.)	50	8	Corned beef	3 oz.	185	0
Flour, all-purpose (sifted)	1 cup	420	80	Frankfurter	1	170	1
Flour, corn meal	1 cup	440	91	Ground beef	3 oz.	245	0
Flour, whole wheat	1 cup	400	85	Ham, baked	3 oz.	245	0
Muffin	1	120	17	Ham, boned	3 oz.	203	0
Rolls, hard	1	155	30	Lamb chop	3 oz.	300	0
Rolls, plain	1	120	20	Pork chop	3 oz.	340	0
Waffles	1	205	27	Pork loin roast	3 oz.	310	0
Pancakes	2 (4")	120	18	Pork sausage links	2	125	trace
Pasta and Rice				Veal cutlet	3 oz.	185	0
Converted rice	2/3 cup	120	27	Veal roast	3 oz.	230	0
Egg noodles	2/3 cup	132	25	**Seafood**			
Macaroni	2/3 cup	127	26	Cod	3 oz.	145	0
Spaghetti	2/3 cup	103	21	Clams, steamed	3 oz.	45	2
White rice	2/3 cup	150	33	Crab	3 oz.	85	1
Sauce, Preserves, etc.				Haddock	3 oz.	105	4
Brown or granulated sugar	1 tbls.	50	13	Halibut	3 oz.	146	0
Catsup	1 tbls.	15	4	Lobster	3 oz.	81	trace
Dill pickles	1 med.	10	1	Oysters	5 med.	66	3
French dressing	2 tbls.	130	6	Perch	3 oz.	195	6
Honey	1 tbls.	65	17	Salmon	3 oz.	120	0
Jam, jellies	1 tbls.	53	14	**Desserts**			
Maple syrup	1 tbls.	60	15	Angel food cake	1 piece	135	32
Mayonnaise	2 tbls.	200	trace	Brownies with nuts	1 square	95	10
Molasses	1 tbls.	45	11	Chocolate cake	1 piece	235	40
Olives	5	30	1	Chocolate chip cookies	2	100	14
Soups				Cupcake	1	90	14
Beef broth	1 cup	30	3	Danish pastry	1	275	30
Bean soup	1 cup	170	22	Doughnut	2	250	32
Celery, creamed	1 cup	162	18	Fruitcake	1 slice	55	9
Chicken	1 cup	95	8	Gelatin, sweet	1 cup	140	34
Chicken noodle	1 cup	65	8	Ice cream	1 cup	255	28
Clam chowder	1 cup	80	12	Pie, 2-crust (apple, cherry)	1 piece	350	51
Onion	1 cup	67	5	Pie, 1 crust—lemon	1 piece	305	45
Pea	1 cup	145	21	pumpkin	1 piece	275	32
Tomato, plain	1 cup	90	16	Pound cake	1 piece	140	14
Vegetable	1 cup	80	13	Popsicle	1	70	18
Beverages				Sherbet	1 cup	260	59
Apple juice	1 cup	120	30	Sponge cake	1 piece	195	35
Chocolate milk	1 cup	240	27	White cake	1 piece	250	45
Cola	8 oz.	97	25	**Candies and Nuts**			
Grapefruit juice	1 cup	130	12	Almonds	12	85	3
Malted milk	1 cup	245	28	Caramels	1 oz.	115	22
Orange juice	1 cup	120	29	Fudge	2 oz.	230	41
Pineapple juice	1 cup	135	34	Hard candy	2 oz.	220	56
Root beer	8 oz.	100	26	Marshmallows	1 oz.	90	23
Soda drinks	8 oz.	113	30	Milk chocolate	2 oz.	290	32
Tomato juice	1 cup	45	10	Peanuts	12	70	2
Vegetables				Peanut butter	1 tbls.	95	3
Peppers, green	1/2 large	12	3	Popcorn	2 cups	80	10
Potatoes, boiled	1 med.	65	15	Walnuts	4	100	2

Food	Size	Cal	Carb	Food	Size	Cal	Carb
Sardines	3 oz.	175	0	Dates, pitted	1/2 cup	123	33
Scallops	3 oz.	115	27	Figs	1 avg.	60	15
Shrimp, canned	3 oz.	100	1	Grapefruit	1/2 med.	45	12
Trout	3 oz.	114	0	Grapes	1 cup	66	16
Tuna	3 oz.	170	0	Lemon juice	1/2 cup	30	15
Poultry				Oranges	1 med.	65	16
Chicken, broiled	avg. serv.	100	0	Peaches	1 med.	35	10
Chicken, canned	3 oz.	170	0	Pears	1 med.	100	25
Chicken pot pie	8 oz.	535	42	Pineapples	1/2 cup	38	10
Turkey	3 oz.	162	0	Plums	1 med.	25	7
Dairy Products				Strawberries	1/2 cup	28	7
Bleu cheese	2 oz.	210	2	Watermelon	1 med.	116	28
Butter	1 tbls.	100	trace	**Vegetables**			
Buttermilk	1 cup	90	12	Asparagus	1/2 cup	15	5
Cheddar cheese	2 oz.	230	2	Beans, baked	1/2 cup	100	24
Cottage cheese	1/2 cup	130	4	Beans, kidney	1/2 cup	100	21
Cream cheese	2 oz.	214	2	Beans, lima	1/2 cup	85	17
Cream, light	1 tbls.	30	1	Beans, green	1/2 cup	15	2
Cream, heavy	1 tbls.	55	1	Beets	1/2 cup	27	6
Eggs, boiled	1 med.	80	trace	Broccoli	1/2 cup	20	4
Eggs, scrambled w/milk	1 med.	110	1	Brussels sprouts	1/2 cup	28	5
Egg white	1 med.	15	trace	Cabbage, raw	1/2 cup	8	2
Egg, yolk	1 med.	60	trace	Cabbage, cooked	1/2 cup	15	3
Margarine	1 tbls.	100	trace	Carrot	1 med.	20	5
Milk, evaporated	1 cup	345	24	Carrots, cooked	1/2 cup	23	5
Milk, nonfat or skim	1 cup	85	12	Cauliflower	1/2 cup	13	3
Milk, whole	1 cup	160	12	Celery	1 stalk	6	2
Parmesan, grated	2 oz.	260	2	Corn	1 ear	90	18
Sour cream	1 tbls.	25	1	Cucumber	1 avg.	30	6
Swiss cheese	2 oz.	210	2	Eggplant	1/2" slice	25	4
Yogurt, skim	1 cup	166	14	Lentils	3 1/2 oz.	106	18
Fresh Fruits				Lettuce	1/4 head	45	3
Apples	1 med.	70	18	Mushrooms	1/2 cup	20	3
Apricot	3 med.	55	14	Onions, cooked	1/2 cup	30	7
Avocado	1 med.	370	13	Peas, cooked	1/2 cup	58	12
Banana	1 med.	100	26	**Other Fruits**			
Blueberries	1/2 cup	44	11	Raisins	1/2 cup	240	64
Cantaloupe	1/2 med	60	14	Strawberries, frozen	1/2 cup	103	26
Cherries, pitted	1/2 cup	55	13	Canned applesauce	1/2 cup	115	31
				Canned fruit cocktail	1/2 cup	98	25

Calorie Burn-Off Guide

2-3 Calories Burned Per Minute
Dusting
Sweeping
Ironing
Sewing
Getting dressed
Desk work
Driving
Walking leisurely
Drawing or painting
Playing cards and board games
Knitting
3-4 Calories Burned Per Minute
Making beds
Bowling
Bicycling on level ground, 5 mph
Walking on level ground, 2 mph
Playing guitar, piano
Typing
Repairing appliances
Pushing a light lawnmower
Wiping floors
4-5 Calories Burned Per Minute
Volleyball
Horseshoes
Bicycling, 6 mph

Gardening
Fishing in still water
Mild exercising
Walking, 2 1/2 mph
Driving a truck
Mopping
Cleaning windows
5-6 Calories Burned Per Minute
Badminton, singles
Tennis, doubles
Swimming, 20 yards per minute
Walking, 3-4 mph
Bicycling, 8 mph
Dancing
Carpentry
Vacuuming
House painting
Paper hanging
6-7 Calories Burned Per Minute
Heavy carpentry
Ice skating
Roller skating
Waterskiing
Horseback riding
Stream fishing
Rope jumping

Vigorous exercises
Walking, 4-5 mph
Bicycling, 10 mph
7-8 Calories Burned Per Minute
Tennis, singles
Skiing
Shoveling snow
Bicycling, 11 mph
Walking, 5-6 mph
Ballet dancing
Square dancing
8-10 Calories Burned Per Minute
Vigorous downhill skiing
Slow jogging, 5 mph
Swimming, backstroke
Bicycling, 12 mph
Digging ditches
Shoveling heavy snow
Climbing stairs
Squash
10-11 Calories Burned Per Minute
Running, 5 1/2 mph
Bicycling, 13 mph
Handball
11-12 Calories Burned Per Minute
Running, more than 6 mph

DIET FORM

Week of	What I Ate	Calories Consumed	Carbo-hydrates
S U N			
M O N			
T U E			
W E D			
T H U			
F R I			
S A T			

Form 13

FITNESS PROGRAM

Week of	Fitness Exercise	Hours Slept	Weight A.M. P.M.	Vitamins
S U N				
M O N				
T U E				
W E D				
T H U				
F R I				
S A T				

BABYSITTER MEMO

Children (names and ages)

_____

_____

_____

_____

We Will Be At (name and phone):

_____

We Will Return at Approximately:

_____

Special Instructions:

Will you do?

_____

_____

The children like (games, TV, books):

_____

_____

Messages

Name: Phone:

_____

_____

_____

_____

Emergency

Doctor: _____ Police: _____

Neighbor: _____

_____

HOUSECLEANING LIST

Regular Chores

	To Do	Com-pleted		To Do	Com-pleted
Kitchen			**Family Room**		
floors	___	___	vacuum	___	___
counters	___	___	dust	___	___
stove	___	___	windows	___	___
refrigerator	___	___	_____	___	___
dishwasher	___	___	_____	___	___
scrub sinks	___	___	_____	___	___
_____	___	___	_____	___	___
_____	___	___			
_____	___	___	**Living Room**		
			vacuum	___	___
Bath (1)			dust	___	___
scrub sink	___	___	windows	___	___
tub	___	___	_____	___	___
commode	___	___	_____	___	___
floor	___	___	_____	___	___
_____	___	___	_____	___	___
_____	___	___			
			Dining Room		
Bath (2)			vacuum	___	___
scrub sink	___	___	dust	___	___
tub	___	___	windows	___	___
commode	___	___	_____	___	___
floor	___	___	_____	___	___
_____	___	___	_____	___	___
_____	___	___	_____	___	___
Bedroom (1)			**Bedroom (2)**		
change linens	___	___	change linens	___	___
vacuum/dust	___	___	vacuum/dust	___	___
floor	___	___	floor	___	___
baseboards	___	___	baseboards	___	___
closet	___	___	closet	___	___
Bedroom (3)			**Bedroom (4)**		
change linens	___	___	change linens	___	___
vacuum/dust	___	___	vacuum/dust	___	___
floor	___	___	floor	___	___
baseboards	___	___	baseboards	___	___
closet	___	___	closet	___	___

General Chores

	To Do	Completed		To Do	Completed
Kitchen			**Miscellaneous**		
clean cabinets	——	——	carpet cleaned	——	——
oven	——	——	draperies	——	——
refrigerator	——	——	telephones	——	——
freezer	——	——	ceiling fans	——	——
wax	——	——	picture frames	——	——
			cobwebs	——	——
Bath			garage	——	——
clean cabinets	——	——			
shower stall	——	——		——	——

Specific for *Your* Home

6

Breaking Your Holding Pattern

*H**ave you ever considered yourself lazy? Oh, come on, be honest. You have, haven't you? I know I* sure have.

We all come out of the womb lazy. People say to me, "Oh, well, you're different. You were born organized."

I'd like to set that fact straight right now. I did not come out of the womb organized. I came out of the womb lazy just like everyone else. In addition, my temperament is one that loves people and variety. If I don't hold myself down, I flit from task to task—always having fun, but not accomplishing much. The difference between how much I get done and how much someone else accomplishes is self-discipline. If a person has the discipline to maintain good organizational habits and be diligent in all he or she does, success is sure to come to that individual.

If I were to ask you what you would prefer to do, what would you answer—clean the stove or lie on the couch eating bonbons and reading a novel? As for me, my *preference* would be the couch, but my *duty* would be the stove.

That will be part of the purpose of this chapter. I want you to see how your planner can help you organize your duties so well that your future will be filled with ample time to enjoy leisurely activities.

HOLDING PATTERNS

One of the greatest benefits the next sections of your daybook will provide will be the systems and techniques for breaking out of whatever holding patterns you now find yourself in.

Most of us truly are locked into holding patterns in life. We have all sorts of justifications for not forging ahead—not enough money, a lack of time, more important priorities—but these justifications only serve as barriers and excuses for our cowardice or lack of direction.

I have a neighbor who completed two years of college before she was married. She intends to finish her degree requirements someday "very soon." The trouble is, she has been saying that for six years now. She's locked in a holding pattern.

I have a relative who read a novel ten years ago about the rural areas of England. Ever since then her big dream has been to take a trip to England, Scotland, and Wales. By now she could have saved the money and gone, but she never bothered to develop a savings strategy. So she now continues to talk of her dream, but with less and less enthusiasm. She's locked in a holding pattern.

I have a girlfriend who has tremendous natural talent in art. She has the best eye for color blends, decorating designs, and pattern matches I've ever seen. She can sketch, paint lovely watercolors, and draw humorous cartoons, and all these skills were self-taught. Her husband wants her to take some business courses at night school and then open her own crafts shop. They've talked about it for nearly three years, yet my friend never enrolls in night school. She claims to be too committed at present to other projects and committees. In truth, I think she's just nervous about taking the big jump into starting a business, and so she stays locked into her holding pattern of doing nothing. By now her store could have been running three years. What a shame.

What about you? What holding patterns are you locked into? What is it that you intend to accomplish one day? What major purchase do you want to make sometime in the future? What risk could you take now but are too hesitant to try?

You read earlier about goals and priorities. Let me encourage you to think back to what you decided then would be worthy goals for you. Take a moment to review them. Were they challenging enough? Are they the sort of ambitious goals that will break you out of your holding pattern? I trust they are, because we are now going to see how your organizer can assist you in reaching those goals.

IT STARTS WITH MONEY

Groucho Marx once said, "Money isn't the only thing in the world, but it sure beats the heck out of whatever is second." Sophie Tucker told a reporter, "I've been rich and I've been poor, and I prefer rich." F. Scott Fitzgerald said to Hemingway one time, "The rich aren't like us, Ernest," to which Hemingway snorted and replied, "I know. They have more money."

People have been talking about money for centuries and have said some very amusing and insightful things about it. Unfortunately, while talk is cheap, nothing else in life is. No one can become an effective life manager without, by necessity, also becoming an effective money manager. The overall design of your organizer must take that into consideration and incorporate several cash-conscious helps.

My husband David has a friend who is a tax attorney and accountant. Although he cannot ethically discuss his clients by name with David and me, he sometimes tells us about the lives of his clients without revealing who they are. Some of the things he relates to us about people's inability to manage money amaze me.

"Can you believe this?" he asked David and me recently. "I just completed a tax return for a man who earns $44,000 annually as an engineer and his wife, a nurse, earns $19,000 a year. They also received an inheritance this year of about $7,000 from a grandfather who died last May. All totaled, they made nearly $70,000 in one year, and they don't have a thing to show for it."

I frowned. "Oh, come on," I protested. "No family can earn $70,000 a year and not have anything to show for it. You're exaggerating surely. They must have two cars or a new house or all new furniture. Be serious."

"I *am* being serious," he insisted. "These people can *make* money, but they just can't manage it. They use credit cards but they don't get around to paying their statements until they are running into the thousands of dollars. By that time the credit card companies have been earning 21 percent interest on the unpaid balance for nearly a year. It costs these people hundreds of dollars in service charges."

David flinched. "What a waste!"

"And it gets worse," our friend insisted. "They give cash donations to charities and their church but never save receipts, so they lose the tax deductions for those donations. And instead of investing in tax-deductible IRAs, which earn high interest, they make random investments in the stock market and waste money on commissions, taxable earnings, and capital gains."

"Stop, stop," I begged, covering my ears. "I can't finish dinner. The very thought of having $70,000 slip through a wife's fingers—*any* wife's—is enough to make me lose my appetite. I'm such a fan of spending."

According to what David's friend tells me, and from what I've had women at my seminars tell me, there are far more household budgets that are out of control than there are budgets under control. I think my old Persian grandpa was right when he used to pull me up on his knee and say, "It's not how much you earn that counts, Donna, it's how you handle what you earn." Right on, Grandpa.

There are three sections of your planner that will help you keep a grip on your hard-earned money.

RECEIPT ENVELOPE

Buy one or more receipt envelopes. These can be placed in any section of the ring binder. I keep mine at the back because mine is usually bulky, but you may prefer to put it near the budget and expenses sheet. We will look at those next. You may need more than one receipt envelope, even as many as one per section.

When you get a receipt, put it immediately into the envelope. You may want to keep a record of the receipts on the outside if time permits. If not, take them out at the end of the month and record them, then discard the receipts or put them where you can retrieve them for the proper purpose.

I never record my receipts on the outside of the receipt envelope, since I have a list of my business expenses on the expenses form (with a receipt envelope just behind it), my grocery shopping on the household budget form (again a receipt envelope follows it), and my personal expenses on the itemized expense form (followed by still another receipt envelope). Listing the receipts again on the receipt envelope would just duplicate these other forms. However, you may not wish to use the other forms, and, therefore, you will list the receipts on the outside of the receipt envelope.

At Christmas I use two receipt envelopes for purchases, and then I do list the items on the outside: a glass whale for Anissa's whale collection, a weed trimmer for David, a blouse for my mother. If a gift needs to be returned, I know exactly where the receipt is located.

When I think of this subject, my mind often jumps back to a time when I was in high school. The wool skirts and matching cashmere sweaters were in style, remember? We were quite poor and our budget didn't stretch far enough to buy those kinds of things, but my mother went all out and bought me a pink skirt and a pink cashmere sweater for Christmas. It was beautiful and I loved it, but the sweater was too big. And I didn't have the receipt. Mistake number two was that I wore the sweater when I boarded the bus to go back to the store and exchange it. Needless to say, the store wouldn't take it back, I got stuck with the sweater and I wore it for a long time to come, baggy as it was. Today, I know better than to wear an item to the store to exchange it, and I now use my receipt envelope to keep all receipts.

Using two receipt envelopes is another idea. Some women keep one for household items and one for business. This system works well at our house. My husband, David, is a stickler for tax preparation. The two-envelope system enables us to prepare for April 15 each month of the year. I have gotten so good at keeping receipts David even pats me on the back for my efficiency. He did laugh, however, when he found a receipt for 64 cents in the envelope. "Donna, you don't have to be *that* organized!"

Household Budget Sheets and Itemized Expenses Sheets

Working with the receipt envelopes as money monitors are the household budget sheets (Form 17 at the end of this chapter) and the itemized expenses sheets (Form 18 at the end of this chapter). The household budget sheets cover all major cash outlay areas from doctor and dentist bills to car and house payments. There is also a miscellaneous section where you can record specific costs that may apply only to your budget (newspaper carrier, club dues, children's allowances, TV repair call). Maintaining such careful records will not only enable you to gauge your monthly budget needs, it will also help you add up grand totals at the year's end. At that point you can say, "Our savings program is too inconsistent" or "The constant repair bills we are getting on the car prove that it's time to trade it in."

If you travel, the expenses forms will be a precise and orderly way to keep track of your expenses. These forms will greatly reduce your tax preparation time, especially when combined with your household records and categorized receipt envelopes. When you walk into the office with organized and accurately kept records, your tax accountant will fall in love with you.

If you do not travel, use the expenses pages for major purchases that do not fall under your household budget, such as a new chair, school clothes, football equipment, soccer uniforms, lawn furniture, or new curtains for the breakfast nook. A review of this list as well as the household budget for the month will give you a better understanding of how you are spending your money. If you will make the effort to keep itemized records of all expenses, you will become more aware of why your savings account isn't growing.

FROM MONEY TO MOTIVATION

The goal section (Form 19) of your planner is where you put onto paper all the concepts we have discussed so far. Everything on these pages pertains to you: who you are, what you want to accomplish, the direction in which you are headed. Do not put all your goals on one page. Place your life's goal and Life Phrase on one page, your five-year goals on another page, your one-year goals on yet another, and your monthly and temporary goals on additional pages. It will work better when they are separate, for the short-term goals will be accomplished faster and more often. You will change your goals from time to time, perhaps move them from one level to another. You will move the achieved ones out, put new ones in, discard some, and write new ones as you grow and expand in your daily life. Keep this section flexible and expandable—and worn from reviewing.

Sometimes you will accomplish one goal and this will change another. For instance, I have always tried to have good posture, ever since a teacher said to me, "All beautiful women have good posture. It's a joy to watch them walk into a room!"

I was such an awkward and plain kid that I have always believed she told me that because she thought at least good posture would make Donna's appearance more appealing.

A few years ago I realized I had begun to slouch, so I wrote "Improve posture" at the bottom of my one-year goal pages. Every time I looked at those words I automatically stood up straight. My posture did improve. That fall, when I listed aerobic exercises as one of my yearly goals, I could eliminate posture, since I already had that area under control. Achieving one goal modified another.

Remember that if you write your goals and never read them, you will forget them. Reading them often gives you direction for your daily activities and a focus for your energy. Your goal section helps you to set your priorities, which will be written and reflected in every other section of your daybook, from the monthly calendar to the record of your monthly financial giving. Having your planner with you at all times will give you many opportunities to review your goals instead of reading the 1978 *Reader's Digest* at the doctor's office!

Person-to-Person Forms

The people section of your planner is for forms marked "Person-to-Person" (Form 20). Here is a place to jot down those reminders of what you wanted to tell a special person, family member, or business associate.

I have a friend whose mother-in-law lives far away in another city. Many times from day to day my friend would think of things she wanted to tell her mother-in-law the next time she called. When the call would come, she could never bring to mind all of those terrific things she was going to share about the grandchildren—the school programs, the little funny things that occurred since she had last spoken to her.

After she started using a daybook, she began to use one of the forms in the person-to-person section just for this purpose. She put her mother-in-law's name at the top. Every time she thought of something to tell her, she wrote it down. Sometimes it was just a word or two to remind her of an incident or event. Now when she calls, my friend opens her book and brings her mother-in-law up to date on the home run her grandson hit in the last softball game and her granddaughter's latest swimming time. This sharing enhances their relationship and cheers Grandma. If you correspond regularly with someone, you may want to adopt this idea.

If you are the chairman of a committee, use these pages to list the suggestions you have for a member of your committee. If you are in business, use this page to list the things you want to discuss with the boss or bring up at the next meeting. Use these pages to keep notes on the positive and negative qualities you see in your employees' performances. When you meet with them individually, you will be able to compliment them on certain areas and suggest improvement in others. The employee will respond to correction better because you have taken the time to observe his or her work closely.

If you set aside a certain time each week to spend with your children individually, this form will help make this hour or two more effective. Put each child's name at the top of one of these pages. Keep notes on what you wish to discuss, the questions you want to ask, the subjects that will draw him or her out. Often we see our children do or say little things in public that we ignore to keep from embarrassing them. Make a note on the child's page. Then approach the child with love. Don't open your planner and lay it on the table and then go down your list, which gives the impression that you watch the child's every move. Review your notes before you take him or her for ice cream. Bring these matters up in the course of conversation when it seems comfortable.

This form has other applications. Use it for prayer requests and to keep track of your gift giving. Create a daily diary/journal that can be transferred to a storage notebook and passed on to your children someday. In a later chapter, which deals with the subject of organizing your work and love, I will suggest other ways to use this section of your planner.

TURNING YOUR DREAMS INTO REALITY

The project planner forms (Form 21) reflect your interests and major commitments. Are you in charge of projects for work, school, or church? Do you end up being chairman of the club, head of various committees, secretary, treasurer, or overall hard worker? This form will help you do the job you have been asked to do and complete it efficiently.

Don't let the word *project* overwhelm you. Your lifestyle will define the word. *Project* can also mean upcoming party, a craft or hobby, a family wedding, a reunion, or the remodeling of your house. The form will bring any size project under control and keep it on target.

Fill in the top section with the basic information, including the purpose of the project or the ultimate goal. Rereading this purpose as you work through the task will keep you action-oriented. Next, put into words the main theme or idea of what you are working on. Think creatively, write down all your ideas, even if they seem foolish. Many of them will be usable once you've modified them slightly.

Work through the available resources for the project and set a clear plan of action to accomplish your goal. Your contacts, committee members, and others who provide services should be listed on the back with their telephone numbers. Materials to purchase, decorations to be made, and programs to be printed should be listed, dated, and checked off as you go. Work out your budget and keep accurate records of your expenses in the space available.

Cross-reference these important dates into your monthly calendar and today pages, making sure you are constantly aware of the progress and deadlines for each project. When the project is complete, remove the page and store it. You may work on a similar project someday or work with the same people. You may need to remember who did the printing, who gave you the best prices on supplies, or where you found costumes or holiday decorations.

New concepts and methods often occur to creative people at the strangest times and in the oddest places. Your notes section (Form 22) is the place to record all of these items, for these are the most difficult to remember, recapture, or re-create. Review them regularly and be inspired by your own ideas.

Use this section in the classroom for lecture notes, on Sunday morning for Sunday school notes, or in seminars and workshops you choose to attend. When you run across an article in a magazine or newspaper that is useful to you, have the article reduced and insert it into your note section. I have notes, copies of articles, and outlines that I have carried in that section for a long time. They are not storage items but things that I am still trying to digest and apply to my life. Once I've learned the concept, I file the material away. I never let the notes section become cluttered. This is an action-filled part of my daybook, which feeds good ideas into every aspect of my life.

A PORTABLE TELEPHONE BOOK

A telephone can be your best friend or worst enemy,

depending on how you control it. If you make use of toll-free (800) numbers to save time on research, then it's useful. If you use the phone to order two tickets to Saturday's production of *Romeo and Juliet* instead of standing in line all afternoon at the box office, then it's useful. However, if you allow your friends to interrupt your planning time or personal family time with a call just to chat, then the phone is harmful. You must control your phone.

In order to be able to contact the key people in your life, your daybook needs a private telephone directory (Form 23). The telephone directory is designed to hold the numbers you need when you are away from home. The purpose is to have crucial numbers when you are standing in an airport, a service station, convention hall, or department store. This section is for the most part used conventionally. However, you can adapt it in different ways. For instance, you can use your telephone directory as a mini-filing system. Janet, an editor friend of mine, always recorded telephone conversations and her notes from meetings on a pad of paper in her leather notebook. One sheet might contain the details of a conversation for one project, the production costs for another book, and the royalty agreement for still another. Every time she needed a specific fact, she had to go through all these pages to first find the fact and then transfer it to another paper, which could be filed in the proper folder in her file cabinet.

Now my friend writes the notes from meetings in the people section of her notebook and the facts (production costs, artists, free-lance writers) for a particular book in the project section; then she transfers these pages to the proper portion of her telephone directory: *J* for that conversation with author Tom Jones, *A* for the book *After the Dance*. Eventually these pages will be stored in the files in her cabinet.

YELLOW PAGES

The section marked "My Yellow Pages" (Form 24) is a terrific addition to any planner. Label your sections according to topic. These yellow pages become your own private resource department, saving you the headache of going through the same process time and time again. For example, you might label one page Child Care, and there list the names and telephone numbers of several reliable babysitters and a local daycare center. Or you might label another page Appliances and list your repairmen—the heating and air-conditioning man, the plumber, the electrician, the general fix-it guy, and anyone else who belongs in that category, with their addresses and telephone numbers.

The next time something breaks down, go to your own yellow pages. Use the people you have used before who have given you good service. Don't lose their telephone numbers. Don't forget their company names and waste time trying to find or remember them.

This section will become more and more valuable to you as you begin to add categories and pull together names and contacts that can help you in various parts of your life.

OVERVIEW

Remember, you are the creator of your own planner/organizer. Select the forms that will be useful to you. Arrange them in an order that works best for you. Your "mind" will function best when it is organized by you. Just one word of caution. My editor friend would never have realized the value of the person-to-person pages, the project pages, and a notepad if she had not experimented with every form for a couple of months. I suggest that you do the same. You might even throw away the many scratchpads on your desk and use your daybook for long memos, just as she did. A slight waste of money, maybe, but a great saving in time and efficiency.

Now you have all the basic information you need to begin using your organizer/planner. Make it more than just a tool of organization. Make it a time-saver, an asset to your life, a creator of extra minutes for enjoyment and relaxation. Let it be your memory. Learn to use it so that your mind will be free to think creatively, productively, and lovingly. Every industry needs tools. The baker needs an oven, pastry brushes, and pans. The carpenter needs a saw, a tape measure, and a hammer. The classroom teacher needs books, pencils, and a chalkboard. Every man and woman needs a daybook.

HOUSEHOLD BUDGET

Rent/ Mortgage Payment	Utilities	Food	Taxes	Insurance: Health and Life
Totals				

Auto Payment	Auto Repair and Gas	Telephone	Clothes	Credit Card	

Child Care	Doctor	Dentist	Rx	Taxes
Totals				

Donations	Savings	Installment Payments	Miscellaneous
Totals			
Monthly Grand Total _____			

ITEMIZED EXPENSES

Name						Week Ending	
Date							
	SUN	MON	TUE	WED	THU	FRI	SAT
From							
To							
To							
Auto Mileage							
At ¢ Per Mile							
Auto Rental							
Gas Oil Lube							
Hotel							
Breakfast							
Lunch							
Dinner							
Air Rail Bus							
Local Cab Bus							
Phone							
Entertainment							
Misc. Tips							
Tolls							
Child Care							
Daily Total							
Total Expenses							

Entertainment (date, who discussed)

Signed:

Itemized Expenses

Date	Item		Amount	
		Total		

GOALS AND PROJECTIONS

	Time Period		
	Items to consider listing: Personal, Physical, Family, Spiritual, Career or Work, Financial	**Target Date**	**Completed Date**

PERSON-TO-PERSON

Record important words or thoughts
to share or remember.

Person or Group

Date	Subject

PROJECT PLANNER

	Project

Start _____ Target _____ Finish _____

Purpose _____

Idea/Summary

Plan *Main Steps* | *Time Required*

Required Resources

Persons *Contacts, Services*   **Phone**

Materials

Budget *Expenses*

	Total		

Form 21, page 2

NOTES

TELEPHONE DIRECTORY

	Telephone
	Address

Name	
	Tel. No.

Name	
	Tel. No.

Name	
	Tel. No.

Name	
	Tel. No.

Name	
	Tel. No.

Name	
	Tel. No.

Name	
	Tel. No.

Name	
	Tel. No.

Name	
	Tel. No.

Name	
	Tel. No.

Form 23

MY YELLOW PAGES

Name

Tel. No.

Name

Tel. No.

Name

Tel. No.

Name

Tel. No.

Name

Tel. No.

Name

Tel. No.

Name

Tel. No.

7

Notes to Nudge Your Memory

WANTED: One glass bowl. Beautiful, useful, and lost. Lent to someone, left somewhere . . . not quite sure where. Owner: Donna Otto, teacher of life management and organization. Please return without any cute comment.

*Yes, I, too, occasionally have problems with disorganization; a daybook has not fully pre*pared me for everything I must cope with in life. I resolve such problems quickly, however. I simply develop a new form, which in the future will handle this new problem. The nice thing about a daybook is that it can be personalized any way you wish. Its function is to meet *your* unique needs, no matter what they may be.

In this chapter I will give you examples of additional forms that can expand your daybook, tailoring it to more specific types of organization. If you choose to make your own forms, take a piece of 8½ x 11 inch paper and draw lines, boxes, or columns in black ink to fit a particular need (some computer programs may also cooperate!). Then take this "camera-ready copy" to a local quick-print shop. The printer will reduce your original and run as many copies as you need quite inexpensively. You can punch holes in these forms and you will have expanded your daybook to fit your individual needs.

If you find forms you like from other sources that don't fit your daybook, your printer can reduce or enlarge these forms to the right size and then run additional copies for you. A variety of colored papers and inks can be used if you wish to delineate forms by color. If you are involved in one of the many service organizations such as Girl Scouts, United Way, or Junior Achievement, you may find it convenient to have certain forms from the organization's handbook, mailing lists, or by-laws reduced and copied for insertion into your daybook.

Now let's review some of the supplemental forms you might wish to add to your daybook. I have organized these forms under four different categories: *time management, personal and family management, business management,* and *church life*. If a couple of them interest you more than others, you can skip a section and go on to the next.

TIME MANAGEMENT

January through December
Dividers with Tabs

I mentioned these dividers earlier. If you use your monthly calendars frequently or like to work six months to a year ahead in your social or business planning, you will find divider pages (Form 25 at the end of this chapter) very practical. Often my speaking engagements are booked far in advance, so the monthly tabs make it easy for me to flip to the month quickly when I'm on the phone or in a meeting and need to scan my schedule in a hurry. If you wish, you can make these dividers very easily at home out of a light card stock cut to size and a tab you glue on the side. Label the tab extension, punch holes, and place it in your notebook section at the appropriate location.

You can also write monthly birthdays and anniversaries on these dividers, so you will always have a record of them. As I mentioned in the last chapter, these dividers are not thrown away, like the month-at-a-glance pages; they remain in your daybook until the corners are so dog-eared they must be replaced.

Week-at-a-Glance Forms

If you are employed outside of the home and you do not have room to combine both your personal and work schedules on your monthly or today pages, you can use the week-at-a-glance forms (Form 26 at the end of this chapter) just for work appointments and business meetings.

My friend Sue is a music instructor. She blocks out the hours of two to five o'clock each afternoon for private lessons on her month-at-a-glance calendar. Then she uses the additional weekly calendars for scheduling individual lessons: "2:00: Johnny Graves (399-8274), 2:30: Jean Thompson (888-7510)." Nothing else goes on her week-at-a-glance forms. Her family and social activities are written on her today pages, again with the afternoon hours, 2:00 to 5:00, blocked out on the days she teaches.

The week-scan forms are also ideal for young people. My daughter, Anissa, used weekly forms instead of today pages to record all of her school assignments for the week (until she graduated from college and began her own business).

If you own a small business and work out of your home, you may wish to record incoming and outgoing orders, pickup items, sales meetings, workshops, seminars, and appointments.

PERSONAL AND FAMILY MANAGEMENT

Travel Packing Checklist

The travel checklist (Form 27) is set up in a format that

not only helps you remember what to pack, but how to coordinate the outfits you are packing. Note the columns where you can designate the colors of your clothes and accessories.

I know how irritating it can be to forget an important item. A couple of years ago David and I went to a lovely hotel in Durango, Colorado, for the weekend. Everything was just perfect, until David joined me in the hotel dining room for breakfast (I was up early and had taken a walk around the gardens). He looked handsome in his dark blue suit, a matching paisley tie, and his new black loafers. Then I saw the white cotton socks.

"Why didn't you wear your dark socks?" I asked when he sat down.

"I would have," he replied, "if you had packed them."

We all have moments like this when we are far from home and find we have forgotten a hair dryer or pantyhose or the dress for a banquet. With a travel checklist, I can pack everything I need in a half-hour. And I can work on my travel list anywhere. If your schedule is full, and you are planning two trips simultaneously, use separate forms with destinations marked on each to plan your trips.

Camping Checklist

If you enjoy camping, as our family does, you might want to add a camping checklist (see Form 28). A master equipment list eliminates the normal hassle of packing. Included are sublists for food and kitchen utensils, clothing, shelter, toiletries, medical supplies, and miscellaneous odds and ends like maps and fire or fishing permits.

Auto Maintenance/Repair Record

This form is designed to serve the meticulous or forgetful person, the single woman, or the person, like myself, who knows nothing about cars except that good maintenance is essential. The form (Form 29) records pertinent auto information: the model, make, and year of the car; the automobile dealership (with the salesman's name and the retail price); the warranty information (the number of years and the parts under warranty); the tire facts; the make and the pounds of air required; oil facts; the weight and recommended frequency of change; the service center name and phone number; and the AAA Motor Club number or another emergency towing service number.

On the bottom and back of the page, you can record all repairs (the type of work that was done and the cost), oil changes, and routine checkups. You might want to put a receipt envelope behind this page so you will have the bill handy if the work is not correct. The combination of records and receipts has helped us sell our cars!

Appliance Record

An appliance record form (Form 30) will help you keep track of the make, model, serial number, year, warranty, and service center of each of your appliances. If some of your appliances are no longer under warranty, write in the name of your appliance repairman. Having this information handy when you call for a service appointment will save the time that a serviceman spends going back to the shop for the proper parts. You pay dearly for repair time, so don't waste it. Also, if you are on a skiing vacation and call the next-door neighbor, who is watching your house, only to hear the distressing words, "Your furnace broke down," you will have the name and number of your favorite serviceman handy.

When we bought our refrigerator, I was unaware that the tray for the icemaker had silicon coating and needed to be replaced periodically. The first time the ice maker malfunctioned, I spent $40 for a service call. The serviceman told me that the tray could be purchased at the appliance store for $6. Believe me, my appliance form now lists the model and serial numbers of the refrigerator, plus the part number for this tray.

Medical Records

The medical records form (Form 31) provides space for all vital medical information for family members: blood type, medications used regularly, any medical condition such as diabetes or hay fever, and any allergies to particular medications. Each person's doctors and their telephone numbers are listed.

There are three columns to record appointments and examinations for these health care areas: *eye, physical,* and *dental.* List the date of your last examination or office visit, the purpose of the appointment, the doctor's instructions, and the date of the return visit. These records answer questions such as: "When did I have my last eye examination?" and "When did Shelley have her last tetanus shot?"

In addition, these forms have space to record each child's immunization records, childhood diseases, and allergies. You will use this information over and over again for soccer teams, summer camps, swimming instruction, and school health records.

Rose Kennedy, mother of the well-known Kennedy clan of nine children, kept a file of 3 x 5 inch cards that listed medical information for each of them. When John F. Kennedy injured his knee as an adult, he was able to consult this permanent record to learn of previous injuries that had weakened his knee and the treatment he received.

Credit Card Record

This form (Form 32) has a place to record the credit card name, the company's address, the credit card number, and the telephone number to call for information or in case the card is stolen. List all this information for each credit card you have, even if you don't use the card often. When you are sending letters to a company about a billing error, shopping by phone, making hotel or airline reservations, or filling out forms for a loan application, this form is quite handy. Recently my wallet was stolen, but between this list and computerized telephone services, I was able to contact and request new cards in less than an hour!

But what if my daybook is stolen? you are wondering. The thief has all the information he or she needs. I suggest that you use a code system to record this information. For example, write the credit numbers above or below the information to which they actually belong. Make a note of this somewhere else in your book so you always remember your system. Let me show you how this works:

Master Card	C.C.	B19476
Standard Oil	C.C.	0-758-K-9654
Penney's	C.C.	J-65458
Sears	C.C.	B-19801-432-90
Visa	C.C.	886641098-W-01

This person's Visa Card number is actually B 19476, which is listed as the Master Card number. The Master Card number is 0-758-K-9654, and so on. Under the letter C (for credit cards) in this person's telephone index are written the words "C.C. down one."

Obviously if many people read this book, this particular code will be broken. You will want to find your own code, or at least adapt this one, to confuse the would-be-thief.

Gift List

This is a general gift list (Form 33) that includes birthdays, weddings, showers, baby gifts, graduation gifts, promotion remembrances, or hostess gifts. This list has places for names, addresses, occasions, gifts purchased, and costs of the items.

You can cross-reference a notation to purchase the gift onto your today pages under the "To Buy" section, so you will be reminded of the upcoming event. When the gift has been mailed or delivered, check it off your gift list. Put a receipt envelope in this section to hold the receipts for these gifts only. When a sweater doesn't fit or a vase gets broken in the mail, your receipt will be right beside the record of the gift.

Christmas Gift List

This form (Form 34) can go in a section of your daybook labeled "Gift List" or a special Christmas section. You will probably want a separate sheet for each family member, and then a sheet for close friends, business associates, and those whom you only remember in some small way. (We will discuss exciting gift ideas for Christmas as well as organization of the holidays later.)

Indicate the year, the person's name, and the gift (where it was purchased and the price) on the front of this form. Once again use a receipt envelope behind this page. Insert all receipts pertaining to the items on that list. When you remove these forms from your daybook after Christmas, store them in one of your standardized binders labeled "Christmas," so you can refer to them next year.

You can use the back of the Christmas list form to record gifts you receive. I keep a record of the name of the sender, the address, the gift I received, and whether or not a thank-you note has been sent. This is also a great way to help your children keep track of the gifts they received and will encourage them to write thank-you notes.

Guest List

If your husband's job or your own job requires you to do a lot of entertaining, or if you personally like to have big parties, a guest list sheet (Form 35) will help you focus on five major areas of concern: the guest list, the guests' telephone numbers, the date the invitations were mailed or an invitation was extended by phone, the response from each person contacted, and a checklist for name tags and/or place cards.

If you are placed on a committee to help organize a church social, a wedding reception, a golden anniversary party, a bowling league banquet, or a political fund-raiser, you will get more accomplished if you divide the large guest list into five parts and assign one part to each committee member. Give each person a copy of these forms and ask them to return them to you (filled in) one week later. You then will have an accurate record of who will and who won't be attending the event and also a system that makes each committee member accountable for her share of the work.

Hospitality/Entertainment Helper

This form will help you keep track of your entertainment plans, from small dinner parties to large group affairs. Record the date, the guest list, and the kind of function—outdoor barbecue, buffet, or sit-down dinner. The menu, the decorations, the centerpiece, the table linens, and the entertainment—strolling violins, a soloist, or an evening of playing Trivial Pursuit—can also be recorded on this form (Form 36).

Several years ago, David and I met the Grammers, a couple who had just moved to Phoenix. We decided to help them get established in the area by introducing them to 50 couples, five at a time. Ten parties! Was I losing my mind? I would have—if I hadn't used ten of these forms, labeled "The Grammer Gathering 1, 2, 3, etc." to keep a running tally of everyone we invited and when they were to come.

This form can also be used for more casual entertaining to help remind you of whom you have recently invited to your house, and how long it's been since you've seen others. It will keep you from serving the same menu to the same people. If you don't have much experience in entertaining, it may also help you get started, acting as your director.

Some of you may be thinking, *She's got to be joking. I don't have time for hospitality.* I know how you feel. In the months I spent writing this book, I had little free time for entertaining. I missed the backyard barbecues and frequent contacts with friends. I finally scheduled some time for entertaining. If you block out one evening a month, you'll be able to enjoy the warmth of entertaining friends and loved ones in your own home or apartment. Try it, you'll like it!

Items Lent and Borrowed

This is where I should have listed the glass bowl referred to in the ad that opened this chapter. (Maybe enough of my friends will read this book so that the bowl will be returned someday.)

I'm sure most of us have had the experience of lending a book, a casserole dish, or a garden tool and never having it returned. This form (Form 37) will help you keep a record of what you lend, so these things are not lost forever.

I've found that when a friend watches me record the name of a book I am lending to her, she remembers to return it.

BUSINESS MANAGEMENT

Client/Contact/Customer Record List

This form (Form 38) is designed for salespeople, so they

can keep an accurate record of referrals, new contacts, and clients. There is space to record name, address, and telephone number. The best hours of the day to contact this person and who referred him or her to you can also be noted. The bottom of the form is for miscellaneous notes, such as the date and size of the subsequent order.

Call Record

If you sell by phone, take pills, do sales follow-up confirmations, or if you are asked to make numerous calls for the Booster Club, small Bible studies, or the PTA, this form (Form 39) will help you write reports and organize your information in your planner rather than on small pieces of paper.

Come up with your own code under the follow-up section so that you remember the response you received from your call and if you need to call again. For example try: LM (left message), LB (line busy), NA (no answer), WCB (will call back). When your sheet is complete and all the calls are made, you can hand it in as a report of what you have done and the response you received, making a copy if you need one.

CHURCH LIFE SERIES

I want to end this list of supplementary forms with several I feel are valuable if you are involved in church activities.

Sermon Notes

Some Christians take their Bibles to church and write sermon notes in the margin. Others are timid about writing in a Bible. I like to use the sermon notes form (Form 40) to take notes in church; then I transfer this form to the back of my daybook. When I need help with a particular subject—depression, marriage, advice to parents—I look back there. At the end of the year I store these forms in my standardized binder, so I can refer to them during my devotion time or in times of needs.

As you can see, you can record the Scripture passages that apply to a particular topic as well as notes about the minister's interpretation. The forms become your own list of inspirational passages, which will help you in times of need. And if you are a Sunday school teacher of either adults or children, you can use this form to note your lesson plan.

Prayer Requests Form

I have always used a prayer list, which puts my needs and the needs of others in black and white so I can pray specifically. Remembering to pray specifically is impossible for me. But writing it down allows me to be a faithful pray-er. I always leave room, as does this form (Form 41), for requests and the outcome.

Add items of thanksgiving to your list. We often become so involved in asking for things, we forget to be grateful for what we already have. We can always afford to focus more on thanksgiving and less on our problems and desires. Be sure to keep the list current.

I store my forms in my binder and the next year get them out and read them. I am always amazed at how God has answered my prayers.

Prayer Journal

This form (Form 42) is a record of your formal prayer time, which we will examine in a separate chapter. We all approach God in a different manner. Each of us brings our own personality, set of circumstances, and measures of joy or sorrow. We come to God just as we are and speak to Him about how we feel. Sometimes when I'm angry about a difficult situation, I want to ask *why* even though age and maturity usually allow us to ask *what*. Writing those feelings down helps me to release that tension and gain a better perspective of the problem.

After three chapters of overviewing a personal daybook, I'm sure you can see why I have a reward notice in the front of mine. It truly *is* my mind, as well as my arms and legs. A daybook is a very important part of organizing my life—and can be equally as important to you.

No two lives are alike; consequently, no two daybooks will be alike. I want you to have the flexibility you need to make your daybook fill all your personal organizational needs. That is why I am suggesting these special supplemental forms. If any or all appear to fit your mode of life, use them.

You can never be too organized.

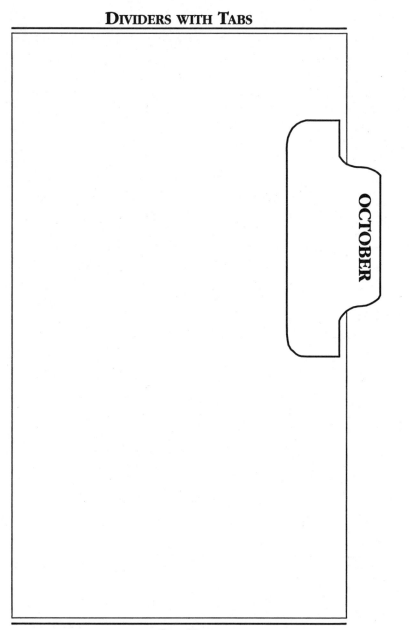

OCTOBER

WEEK-AT-A-GLANCE

Week Scan
(Circle Month)   JAN   FEB   MAR   APRIL   MAY   JUNE

Week beginning

Monday   Date

AM   APPTS   TO DO

NOON

CALLS

PM

Tuesday   Date

AM   APPTS   TO DO

NOON

CALLS

PM

Wednesday   Date

AM   APPTS   TO DO

NOON

CALLS

PM

Week Scan

(Circle Month)   JULY   AUG   SEP   OCT   NOV   DEC

Week ending

Thursday   Date [   ]

AM   APPTS   TO DO

NOON

                                           CALLS

PM

Friday   Date [   ]

AM   APPTS   TO DO

NOON

                                           CALLS

PM

Saturday   Date [   ]   **Sunday**   Date [   ]

Form 26, page 2

TRAVEL CHECKLIST

Apparel:	Color	Accessories:	Color	Undergarments:	
Suits	_____	Ties/Scarves	_____	T-Shirts	_____
	_____		_____	Shorts	_____
	_____		_____	Panties	_____
Jackets	_____	Belts	_____	Slips	_____
	_____		_____	Bras	_____
	_____		_____	**Miscellaneous**	
Dresses	_____	Hats	_____	Camera & Film	_____
	_____		_____	Journal	_____
	_____		_____	Reading Material	_____
Shirts	_____	Jewelry	_____		_____
	_____		_____		_____
	_____		_____	Vitamins	_____
Shoes	_____		_____	Medications	_____
	_____	Hankies	_____	Aspirins	_____
	_____	Stockings	_____		
Handbags	_____			Stationery	_____
	_____	**Sleepwear**		Stamps	_____
	_____	Robe	_____	Recreational	
Shorts	_____	Slippers	_____	Equipment	_____
	_____	P.J.'s	_____		_____
	_____	**Cosmetics**			_____
Slacks	_____	Toothbrush and		Passport	_____
	_____	Toothpaste	_____	Travelers	
	_____	Razor	_____	Checks	_____
		Shaving Cream	_____	Business	
Sport Clothes		Hairspray	_____	Papers	_____
Swimsuit	_____	Makeup	_____		_____
Cover-up	_____	Nail Care	_____		_____
Pool Shoes	_____	Face Creams	_____		_____
Tennis Clothes	_____	Cologne	_____		_____
	_____	Hairdryer	_____	Gifts for	
Running Clothes	_____	Curling Iron	_____	Hostesses	_____
		Curlers	_____		_____

Form 27

BACKPACKING/CAMPING CHECKLIST

Food
- Canteen
- Water Bag or Jugs
- Pots
- Fry Pan
- Cup/Bowl
- Tablespoon/Silverware
- Foil
- Matches
- Pot Tongs
- BP Grill
- Stove Fuel
- Eating Utensils
- Salt/Pepper
- Milk/Sugar
- Coffee/Tea
- Drink Mix
- Cooking Oil
- Trail Snacks

Clothing
- Socks
- Underwear
- Sock Cap
- Pj's/Long Johns
- Jacket
- Wool Shirt
- Windbreaker
- Rainwear/Poncho
- Bandannas
- Swimsuit
- Gloves
- Sneakers
- Shirt
- Trousers
- Shorts

Shelter
- Tent & Stakes
- Sleeping Pad/Air Mattress
- Sleeping Bags
- Ground Cloth
- Nylon Cord
- Tarp

Toiletries
- Toothbrush
- Toothpaste
- Soap
- Toilet Paper
- Towel
- Washcloth
- Sanitary Supplies
- Mirror/Razor
- Contact Lenses Supplies

Medical
- Antiseptic
- Band-Aids
- Gauze Pads
- Moleskin
- Snake Kit
- 2" Adhesive Tape
- Tweezers
- Safety Pins
- Medications
- Sun Lotion
- Glasses
- Vitamins
- Water Purifiers

Miscellaneous
- Matches
- Candles
- Flashlight
- Batteries
- Plastic Bags
- Maps
- Notebooks/Pens
- Fire Permit/Fish Permit
- Camera/Film
- Game/Cards
- _____
- _____
- _____
- _____
- _____
- _____
- _____

Form 28

Auto Maintenance Record

Year: _____ Mfr. _____

Model: _____

Purchased From: _____

Salesperson: _____

Price: _____

Warranty Info: _____

Tire Facts (lbs. of air): _____ brand and type _____

Oil Facts (weight): _____ frequency of change _____

Dealer or Service Center: _____

Phone No.: _____

Service Record

Date	Service	Expense
		$

Service Record

Date	Service	Expense
		$

APPLIANCE RECORD

Appliance: _____

Manufacturer: _____

Model Name and Number: _____

Year: _____

Serial No. _____

Maintenance Policy purchased   yes _____ no _____

Insured by: _____

Name and Number: _____

Appliance: _____

Manufacturer: _____

Model Name and Number: _____

Year: _____

Serial No. _____

Maintenance Policy purchased   yes _____ no _____

Insured by: _____

Name and Number: _____

Appliance: _____

Manufacturer: _____

Model Name and Number: _____

Year: _____

Serial No. _____

Maintenance Policy purchased   yes _____ no _____

Insured by: _____

Name and Number: _____

Form 30

MEDICAL RECORDS

Name: _____ Blood type: _____

Immunizations

Date	Type	Date	Type

Disease Contracted

Date   Type   Details _____

_____

_____

_____

_____

Injuries, Accidents

Date   Details _____

_____

_____

_____

_____

Examination Record

Physical	*Dental*	*Eye*
Date, Checkup, Results	Date, Checkup, Results	Date, Checkup, Results

CREDIT CARD INFORMATION

Company Name Address Phone Number	Exp. Date	No. of Cards Issued	Card Number	Call if Lost or Stolen

Form 32

GIFT LIST

Name _____

Personal Data (Age/Sizes) _____

_____

Occasion _____

Gift Ideas (Interest Area) _____

_____

_____

| Date Sent | Cost | Acknowledged |

Name _____

Personal Data (Age/Sizes) _____

_____

Occasion _____

Gift Ideas (Interest Area) _____

_____

_____

| Date Sent | Cost | Acknowledged |

Name _____

Personal Data (Age/Sizes) _____

_____

Occasion _____

Gift Ideas (Interest Area) _____

_____

_____

| Date Sent | Cost | Acknowledged |

Form 33

CHRISTMAS GIFT LIST

Name _____ Personal Data _____

Ideas _____

_____

19 ___ Sent _____	Cost $_____	Acknowledged _____
19 ___ Sent _____	Cost $_____	Acknowledged _____
19 ___ Sent _____	Cost $_____	Acknowledged _____
19 ___ Rec'd. _____	Cost $_____	Acknowledged _____
19 ___ Rec'd. _____	Cost $_____	Acknowledged _____

Name _____ Personal Data _____

Ideas _____

_____

19 ___ Sent _____	Cost $_____	Acknowledged _____
19 ___ Sent _____	Cost $_____	Acknowledged _____
19 ___ Sent _____	Cost $_____	Acknowledged _____
19 ___ Rec'd. _____	Cost $_____	Acknowledged _____
19 ___ Rec'd. _____	Cost $_____	Acknowledged _____

Name _____ Personal Data _____

Ideas _____

_____

19 ___ Sent _____	Cost $_____	Acknowledged _____
19 ___ Sent _____	Cost $_____	Acknowledged _____
19 ___ Sent _____	Cost $_____	Acknowledged _____
19 ___ Rec'd. _____	Cost $_____	Acknowledged _____
19 ___ Rec'd. _____	Cost $_____	Acknowledged _____

GUEST LIST

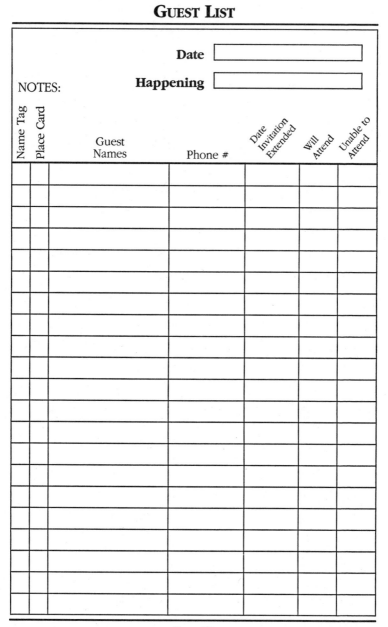

NOTES:

Date

Happening

Name Tag	Place Card	Guest Names	Phone #	Date Invitation Extended	Will Attend	Unable to Attend

Form 35

HOSPITALITY/ENTERTAINMENT HELPER

Happening (Description) _____

_____

_____

Date _____

Place _____

Menu (Beverage, Appetizers, Main Course, Dessert)

_____

_____

_____

_____

Assistants and Caterer

_____

_____

_____

Activities

_____

_____

_____

_____

To Do	Budget
	$

Form 36

ITEMS LENT AND BORROWED

Name of Item/Owner	Date Item Borrowed/ Loaned	Date Returned

Form 37

CLIENT/CONTACT/CUSTOMER RECORD

Name _____ Phone _____

Address _____

City _____ State _____ Zip _____

Referred by _____ Date _____

Notes and Pertinent Information _____

_____

_____

Name _____ Phone _____

Address _____

City _____ State _____ Zip _____

Referred by _____ Date _____

Notes and Pertinent Information _____

_____

_____

Name _____ Phone _____

Address _____

City _____ State _____ Zip _____

Referred by _____ Date _____

Notes and Pertinent Information _____

_____

_____

Name _____ Phone _____

Address _____

City _____ State _____ Zip _____

Referred by _____ Date _____

Notes and Pertinent Information _____

_____

CALL RECORD

Date	Person Phoned	Response

LM (left message)   **LB** (line busy)   **NA** (no answer)   **WCB** (will call back)

SERMON NOTES

Date

Speaker

Subject

Key Reference(s)

		Notes	Verse Ref.

Form 40

PRAYER REQUESTS

		Individual or Group	
Date	Person Requesting		Request/Outcome

Form 41

PRAYER JOURNAL

	Date

Today's Scripture _____

_____

_____

Thank-yous _____

_____

_____

Concerns _____

_____

_____

_____

_____

_____

_____

_____

_____

What's God saying to me? Insights, revelations (in Scriptures or in my conscience)

_____

_____

_____

_____

_____

_____

_____

_____

_____

_____

Form 42

8

Ship Out the Clutter—
Shape Up Your Home!

*We mentioned in the introduction and in chapter
2 the internal desire we all have to be organized.*
We don't always succeed, but we do desire it.

Well, the fact is we *could* succeed if we would rid ourselves of some of the clutter we wade through each day and
simplify some of our most burdensome tasks. That will be
the purpose of these next few chapters. We will examine
the simple and complex operations of your day-to-day life
and offer quick and easy solutions you can put into immediate practice to help you with your household, your
personal care, and your children.

YOUR GREATEST ALLY—
AN EASY-TO-USE STORAGE SYSTEM

Ever look for something you know you had but couldn't
find? This section is for you! Builders design houses with 15
to 18 percent of the space set aside for *active* storage. Often,
however, because of poor organization, we end up using as
much as 35 percent of our living space for storage. This is
not only uncomfortable, it's often a fire hazard or a trap for
stumbling, tripping, or falling over things. You don't want

that. Just as our daybooks are not for storage, neither are our living rooms, kitchens, or cabinets.

What makes you tired? *The things you don't do, not the things you do.* If you don't use a storage system, you will avoid cleaning certain closets and cupboards because they are so messy. The thought of these cluttered areas of your home will nag you just like my Mexican tile nags at me.

Begin your home organization by going through your home room-by-room and getting rid of as many junky items as possible. I take three large black lawn bags and declare war on the mess. One bag is for throwaways. The second is for putaways (items that belong in another room) and treasures that should be stored in the garage or attic (high school yearbooks and craft projects). The third is for giveaways. Sometimes I donate to a garage sale from the throwaway bag or give it to the Salvation Army.

The putaways are quickly returned to the proper areas of my house. The treasures—those memorabilia, travel souvenirs, and Christmas decorations—go into my storage system, a series of identically sized, sturdy storage boxes. These boxes *should not have printing or writing on them.* I began with ten heavy duty cardboard storage boxes (15 x 12 x 10), which I purchased from a stationery store.* That was many years ago. I now have 47 boxes. You, too, can expand your number of boxes as your needs increase—more children, a larger house, new hobbies.

Number the front and side of each box. If more than one box holds related materials, such as three boxes of books, you may wish to number the boxes in alphabetical sequence (7-A, 7-B, 7-C). Use a similar sequence for Christmas items. No matter how many boxes you begin with, start the Christmas boxes with 25 so they may be kept together. (See Illustration 3, next page).

---

* These may also be purchased from the address at the back of this book.

Try packing each box with items that relate to each other. For example, box 18 at our house contains my husband David's high school and college memorabilia. One day before his twentieth high school reunion, he took down this box and pulled out his varsity sweater, class yearbook, photos of his classmates, and old programs from school stage presentations to show me. I enjoyed the reunion because I "knew" his friends, even though they didn't know me. I doubt that David will look at the box again until his fortieth high school reunion, but box 18 will be there when he wants it.

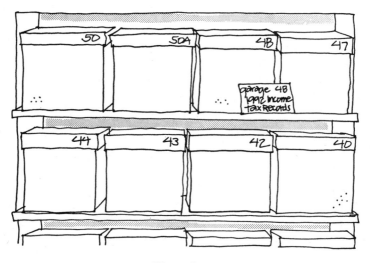

Illustration 3

Once you fill a box, write down on a 3 x 5 inch index card the inventory of everything contained in that box. At the top of the right side of your card put the corresponding box number and on the upper left side a memo to yourself about where the box is stored in your house (see illustration above). Some women fill a box and then cannot remember if it is in the attic, garage, basement, or perhaps in a closet at the lake cottage. Put your packet of index cards in a convenient place where they will be accessible to everyone in the family.

What happens when you want to empty a box? I store craft projects in my storage system, and sometimes my interest in them is renewed and I actually finish one. About ten years ago I started an afghan, which I expected to finish in a month or so. I worked on the afghan for several months, leaving it in a decorative box in our family room. Soon, however, I realized that I was cleaning around that box week after week and only working on the blanket about once a month. That was it.

I put all the afghan components into a plastic bag and stored them in box 15. Four years went by. Then one year I decided, "That afghan would be a great Christmas present for Mother." That July I went to the garage and got the half-finished afghan, with the rest of the yarn and the needle and the instructions. I attacked the project with renewed vigor and had a Christmas present finished by early December.

What happened to box 15? Absolutely nothing. I saved box 15, but I tore up the index card. When I needed a new storage box, I wrote up a new card for box 15.

One additional suggestion about your storage system: I put a red circle or bright star on one or two boxes, which contain absolutely priceless family items, such as photographs, special scrapbooks, or handwritten letters from aged members of the family. Should a fire ever break out in our house, I will grab these boxes on my way out if possible.

If you've ever looked for something you knew you had and finally gave up, looked for something for more than two minutes, or purchased a duplicate of something you knew you had, it need never happen again.

Multiplying Space

Now you are ready to revamp your cleaned storage

space. Obtain a business supply catalog or an office supply order sheet and find out what unique cabinets, bins, and shelf units are available that would work perfectly for the odd nooks and crannies of your home. Be creative in your thinking. For example, a silverware tray or a drawer insert, which is designed to hold paper clips, stamps, thumbtacks, and staples in a desk drawer, would also be a perfect item to keep your rings, necklaces, bracelets, and pins from getting tangled together. It could also be used to separate your cosmetics.

In your clothes closet, mount the rod higher than normal and then drop a chain from the side and the middle of this rod. Connect the two chains with a one-inch wooden dowel, which runs beneath the level of your husband's hanging jackets. This gives you another rod on which to hang a row of shirts (Illustration 4).

Illustration 4

Consider attaching rods and dowels to the back of bathroom doors, linen closets, and bedroom doors so that you can hang towels or tomorrow morning's clothes on them.

To maximize drawer space in your kitchen, purchase (or make from cardboard) dividers which you can use to section off your drawer space. Flat baskets also work well. One section can hold cookie cutters, another section potholders, and another section measuring cups. This not only organizes your implements, it makes full use of whatever drawer space you have available.

Use the total space under kitchen and bathroom sinks for storing home supplies. Buy a metal cabinet with plastic drawers and mount it on an inside garage wall or storage room wall and put small items there. Mount large pegboards on your inside garage walls and maximize that space to hang screwdrivers, wrenches, and other small tools.

Keep in mind that the function of storage space is to relieve you of clutter and to enhance your overall organization.

SYSTEMATIZING KITCHENS

Now that the major decluttering has been accomplished, let's look at ways to make the kitchen, the hub of your home, more attractive and efficient. Kitchens are hard to keep clean of clutter because so many diverse activities take place there. Your *stove-top cooking* requires special pots and pans and protective mittens; your *baking* requires special bowls and mixers and hand utensils; your *cold storage* requires a freezer unit, a refrigerator, plastic containers, and ice trays; your *cleanup* requires a dishwasher, sink, detergents, cloths; and *eating* requires glasses, dishes, silverware, and serving utensils.

What a madhouse of activity! Women tell me, "When friends come for dinner and ask if they can help, I'd like to be able to say yes, but I don't. I'm too embarrassed to have them see my cluttered cupboards and messy refrigerator."

I sympathize with that feeling. I used to feel that way too. Now all my acquaintances want to observe my kitchen cabinets and other closets. "Can I see how you do it?" they ask, partly, I think, so they can pick up new ideas and partly to see if I really practice what I preach. Believe me, my kitchen *is* well organized. Your kitchen can be that way too. Let me give you some organizational tips.

Never Used Items

Begin by inspecting all your small appliances. If some are old and broken, either take them to the repair shop and get them fixed or else throw them out. If you have appliances you never use—two spare coffeepots or a waffle iron that never gets used because your family hates waffles—give these items to your church kitchen on indefinite loan or to a needy family or to a son or daughter who is going off to college or setting up housekeeping for the first time.

Next, inspect every drawer and cupboard for other never-used items and get rid of them too. Why keep 11 aprons when you need no more than two or three? Why keep umpteen zillion extra glasses just because they have the Little Mermaid or Beauty and the Beast on them? Your children can select two or three favorites and then allow you to get rid of the extras and duplicates. Why keep the remaining odd pieces of an old set of dishes? You need the space.

Cupboards

When you organize your cupboards, put seldom-used items way up high and pushed to the back. These items would include serving pieces (especially silver pieces), food coloring, bowls for Christmas cooking, extra salt and pepper shakers, centerpiece vases, pitchers, and platters for serving large portions of meat.

Put the items you use frequently in the easy-to-reach places. These items include salt, pepper, cups, glasses, dishes, silverware, frying pans, spices, and the coffeepot. Try to keep one electric cord, which will fit all your basic appliances, so that your counter will not look like Central Dispatch with wires running all over the place.

I recommend that you totally remove as many items from your kitchen as you can if they are clutter items. Get a storage box, number it, and fill it with your ice bucket, crepe pan, punch bowl and cups, and other superfluous kitchen items. Note on an index card what has been stored and where and then don't worry about it any longer. My rule of thumb is: If I don't use it at least once a month, I need to store it.

Give your drawers and cupboards a thorough cleaning as you organize. Use your vacuum cleaner hose attachment to clean out drawers. Wash everything and then apply adhesive-backed vinyl paper that is color-coordinated to your kitchen. I know it takes a little more time, but vinyl paper is worth installing, since it keeps drawers clean for a long time and is sturdy enough to wash repeatedly.

Unused Space

Try to make use of the air space in your kitchen by hanging wicker baskets on wrought iron or brass utility hangers. I hang all kinds of implements on my utility hanger, such as pots and pans, wire french fry potato baskets, and pot holders. Also on the hangers I put decorative kitchen gadgets and attractive serving spoons. Some people put up new shelves or hang wooden racks under the cabinet to hold long-stemmed glasses upside down. Some types of automatic drip coffeemakers, spice shelves, cookbooks, cookbook holders, and microwaves can be attached under your cupboards so that your counter will have more space.

Most department stores sell rubber drawer dividers and plastic wall hangers that extend from pantry doors.

If you place a decorated crock jar or canister near your stove, it can hold ladles, wooden spoons, whisks, pancake turners, and spatulas. This leaves more space in your kitchen drawers. If an area of your counter is dark, you can buy portable lights, which can be screwed into the bottom of your overhead cabinets.

Junk Drawers

Illustration 5

Everybody has a junk drawer. Believe it or not, they're a necessary part of kitchen organization; they hold those little coffee filters, garbage-bag twist ties, matches, tacks, cellophane tape, and dozens of other small items (Illustration 5). I recommend that you buy a silverware tray and place those items in the various sections. Use an egg carton with the top torn off so that 12 sections are open upward.

Pimento, honey, or jam jars can also hold small items in a junk drawer.

By the way, strive to make junk drawers and junk closets less junky by ridding yourself of carryover items. Don't accumulate packs of matches, dozens of extra brown shopping bags, or unused canning jars. Decide how many brown bags you need and pitch the others. You need the space. Cover some shoe boxes with adhesive-backed vinyl paper to match your drawers and shelves, and use those for your package mixes, such as chili or gravy.

Pantries

When organizing your pantry, use a plastic label maker to label your shelves *Cereal, Coffee, Sugar.* If you have small children who can't read, tape a picture of the object next to the name. In this way, children can put things back where they belong, as well as help you unpack groceries when you come home from the store. Sometimes a young child's natural desire to help Mom is squelched by her saying, "No, you can't help unload the groceries. You don't know where everything belongs." Or more frequently with older children, Mom hears the protest, "I can't help. I don't know where everything goes."

I use a lot of jars in my kitchen, not only on my counter, but also in my pantry. Jars are great since I can easily see what's inside of them—popcorn, beans, and chips. We live in a climate where it's very hot for long periods of time, so I worry about being invaded by all kinds of bugs. Jars are airtight and don't often get as many critters.

I label each jar. I also drop the instructions for the use of its contents inside. For example, if I open a bag of rice and secure it in an airtight jar to keep it fresh, I cut the cooking directions off the bag and tape them to the jar (Illustration 6, next page).

As you reorganize your kitchen, think of this principle:

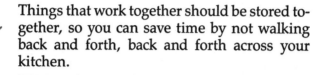

Things that work together should be stored together, so you can save time by not walking back and forth, back and forth across your kitchen.

Illustration 6

I have a galley kitchen. At first it seemed natural to arrange my kitchen with appliances at one end, cords nearby, and nonperishable foods in the pantry at the other end.

One morning I realized that I walked the length of my kitchen twice, which takes approximately one minute, just to make a pot of coffee. What could be changed? Not the faucet, that's for sure. So I decided to put my coffeepot under the sink, the cord in the towel drawer next to the sink, and the coffee in a decorative canister on the counter by the sink. This reorganization saved me one minute a day, six hours in the year. I would rather read a book for six hours than walk across the kitchen for that amount of time.

Put popcorn with the popcorn maker, rolling pins near the bowls. Group things appropriately. Stack and tuck your pots and pans. Use a plate space-saver to store your lids. They stand upright, take up much less space, and move in and out easily.

Remember that your refrigerator and freezer are cabinets. They're just cold cabinets, and, as such, you can keep them in the same kind of order that you keep your other cabinets. Use some of those plastic turntables inside of the refrigerator, just as you use them in your cabinets. If you have a lazy Susan in the center of the top shelf, you can spin it around to get a bottle of ketchup, a cup of yogurt, or a bottle of salad dressing. No longer will you have to try to reach over everything inside. One word of caution: The first few days younger children may want to spin the lazy Susan, so store only a few nonbreakable items on the turntable for the first week.

Your cheese and meats go in the coldest place. You can store eggs in your refrigerator for several months. Try to rotate your eggs in the egg container. If you buy large quantities to store, turn the cartons upside down every so often. Keep a box of baking soda somewhere in the refrigerator to keep the inside smelling fresh. I also recommend that you use zippered plastic bags or some kind of protector to keep items fresh as long as possible. I often make up ground beef patties as soon as I come home from the market. Sometimes I add onions and eggs to the patties at this time, then I place them on a cookie sheet and slip them into the freezer to freeze for 30 to 60 minutes. Now they are ready to store in a zippered freezer bag. Use six patties for spaghetti or ten for meatloaf or as many as needed for hamburgers.

If you like bacon but can't use a whole pound in a week or so, freeze the entire pound. Separate and lay all the pieces in a pound out on a strip of waxed paper, and then roll up the paper like a jelly roll. Freeze it, and then slip the roll into a zippered bag for freshness. When you need a slice or two of bacon for a spinach salad or you need just one or two slices for breakfast, pull off a strip or two and fry them as usual.

More foodstuffs can be frozen than most of us realize. Friends of ours from Louisiana give us five pounds of pecans every year for Christmas. I can't use five pounds very quickly, so I store the nuts in the freezer. What else? Chocolate candy, popcorn, chocolate chips, potato chips, tortilla chips. I like to buy in large quantities to save money, so I store pancake batter flour and corn meal in the freezer, so they will stay fresh.

One day, when our power was out, my husband shouted to me, "Donna, where are the candles?"

"In the freezer," I replied nonchalantly.

"This is not a time to crack jokes!" he said tersely.

"I'm not kidding," I said. "That's where they are." I quickly went to the freezer, took the candles out, and handed them to him.

When the blackout was over, David apologized. "I'm sorry I shouted at you about the candles. But *what on earth* were they doing in the freezer?"

"David, I buy cheap candles. I put them in the freezer so they'll burn longer." (That's true, by the way.)

"Oh," David replied. The approving smile on his face told me he was proud of my thrift.

Anyone can control clutter. It just requires that things be put in their proper places. I stress this concept so much that it's rubbed off on my daughter. Her first complete sentence was, "Put it back where you got it."

Think as you put each item back: Am I storing this as closely as possible to the place where I use this item? Are the mixing bowls closest to the counter where I do most of my stirring and mixing? Are the dishes and the glasses and the silverware near the dishwasher so that as I'm emptying it, I'll be able to store them quickly and efficiently?

Control clutter and stay organized. You'll save energy, money, time, and sanity.

COOKING QUICKLY

While we're in the kitchen area, let's look at some ways you can make your cooking and entertaining tasks easier. There are many ways you can put together delicious, yet simply prepared, daily meals. I'll give you a few ideas. First, however, let me suggest that you do as much creative thinking as possible in regard to saving time cooking. As I am cooking a meal, I continually ask myself, "How could I save time in the future when I prepare this same meal?" You should challenge yourself the same way.

Sometimes I spend Saturday morning cooking four or five different meals at the same time. Then I simply reheat them during the week. I use a lot of cold main dishes, fish dishes, nonmeat dishes, and salads. With these prepared in advance, I just have to add a platter of steamed vegetables. It makes dinner an easier meal to put together.

Breakfast can be an easy meal too. Before going to bed, put various mixtures in your blender and in the morning just whip it together. Sometimes I use eggs, fresh fruit, milk, and vanilla. I also like strawberry ice cream, bran, milk, fresh strawberries, and cinnamon. Meals that are nutritious don't have to have a bad taste.

Another idea is to take a muffin pan with eight cups in it. Put sliced ham into four holes and then break a raw egg over each slice of ham. In the other four cups, put paper muffin cups and pour muffin batter into them, cover and refrigerate—a great job for kids the night before. The next morning just put the muffin tray in a 325 degree oven for 20 minutes. By the time everyone is dressed, breakfast is ready.

Lunches are not difficult to prepare, whether they are eaten at home or packed in a lunchbox or brown bag. Put your leftover stew, soup, or chili into a wide-mouth insulated bottle and send it to work or school with family members. Prepare lots of finger food (carrot sticks, celery sticks, raw cauliflower) once a week and store it in plastic containers for use all week. (Children eat what they see first when they open the refrigerator door.) Vary the sandwiches you prepare by using pita bread instead of sliced bread now and then. Instead of bologna and mustard, make a sliced zucchini with cheese sandwich or a jam and nuts sandwich or a cream cheese sandwich. Be original.

SHOPPING RAPIDLY

To make the most of my time, I never go to the grocery store on Friday night or Saturday. I prefer lunchtime on weekdays or 6:00 any morning. Some women have begun to shop at midnight, now that so many stores are open 24 hours a day.

Look for prices or computer codes on all items you choose so that the checker won't have to call for a price once you get to the check-out counter. If you shop weekly or biweekly, don't get too many perishable items, even though the produce really looks great that week.

When you are shopping, load items together that will later be stored together: frozen foods in one area; staples like flour, sugar, cake mixes in another; foods that need to be refrigerated in another. No doubt, the bagger will bag them the same way. If he doesn't, it's worth asking him to do so. Once you get home, you can put each bag on a counter, close to the proper closet or storage area, and unload your groceries quickly.

When you are selecting recipes, make sure you read the directions before you shop and note them on the grocery form in your daily planner. I seldom select recipes that take four dozen procedures or have to be prepared over a long period of time.

ORGANIZING RECIPES

One thing I've discovered through years of observation is that women are constantly recopying recipe books to fit 3 x 5 inch cards or to put into systems they currently have. I don't do that anymore.

If I clip a recipe from a magazine that I want to save or if someone (such as a favorite relative) gives me a personally handwritten recipe that I want to save in its original form, I store it in a loose-leaf binder. I have an 8½ x 11 inch, three-ring binder filled with clear plastic protectors and a set of dividers that separates "breads" from "meats" from "desserts," and so on (Illustration 7). I don't waste time recopying recipes onto file cards and then saving both copies. That squanders my time and adds to my clutter. I simply staple the recipe, as it is, under the plastic protector, and that protects it and keeps it handy.

Illustration 7

HOSPITALITY

Sometimes we all feel "Entertaining's just not worth it!" For those times I've found some simple, uncomplicated, uncluttered ways to be hospitable, which require minimum time and effort.

"Fix-it-yourself" parties are always fun, since everyone cooks his or her own tacos, wok foods, or baked potatoes with toppings, or fixes a personal sundae. Sometimes I have a sukiyaki (known in Japan as the "friendship dish") dinner where each couple cooks their own meal right at the table in an electric frying pan or wok.

"That doesn't make things easy for me," you say. "I still have to cut up all the meat and vegetables for three couples, which takes as much time as preparing any recipe."

Not the way I entertain. I give my guests a copy of the recipe ahead of time. Each wife cuts up the meat and vegetables for that couple's serving. Then, guess who cooks at the table that night? Usually, the husband. The men love to ham up the role of chief chef while the women watch. I provide aprons and hats to set the tone.

Sometimes I have brunches rather than dinners. A Saturday brunch, a lunch/breakfast meal, is easier to fix and usually isn't as expensive. "All-in-one bowl" parties, where you serve chili or stew or vegetable soup, are inexpensive and fun. Outdoor cookouts are simple too. You can throw the paper plates away and not have to waste time and energy washing dishes.

And don't forget about potluck dinners. I'm not embarrassed to call a friend and say, "We've really missed you two. How about getting together Friday night. Could you bring a salad? The Davises are coming, and Carolyn is bringing dessert. I'll make the main course, and we can have a good time together." Remember, people are more interested in being with you than they are in eating a fancy Chateaubriand dinner.

SORTING LAUNDRY

If cooking is one major household task that responds almost miraculously to some simple organizational tricks, doing laundry is another. There are several ways to save steps when you tackle the family's laundry. One idea is to put large dishpans in the laundry room, each one labeled with a different family member's name on it. As you sort the clean laundry, put it in the appropriate dishpan. Each family member is then responsible for picking up his or her own clothes, folding and carrying them to the bedroom, and putting them away. You may have to fold clothes for your younger children.

You should remind each family member not to put clothes in the clothes hamper if socks or T-shirts or other items of clothing are turned inside out. Explain to everyone that it adds needless work on your washday for you to have to pull everything rightside out again. (If they forget, simply wash the clothes inside out and return them that way. Next time they'll remember.)

It also helps to put a laundry bag in each person's bedroom so that children are encouraged to put their dirty clothes in the bag rather than leaving them lying on beds, the floor, or the dresser. The person responsible for gathering the week's clothes can either go room to room combining clothes in one laundry bag or he can take all the bags to the laundry room.

As you dole out jobs among family members, remember to assign sock sorting to a younger child. Hand laundry can be done in a sink with a preschooler swishing it around until it is clean. Give up ironing altogether. Use small loads in your dryer and get the clothes out when you hear the buzzer. If I have to let a load sit after the dryer is finished and a blouse is wrinkled, I throw it back into the dryer with a wet towel. It may be expensive to run the dryer that extra time, but you avoid the time it takes to iron the blouse.

I love to dry my clothes outside most of the year. A lady once taught me how to avoid that stiff texture, which is especially noticeable in your towels. Even the heaviest velour towel will stay fluffy if I throw it into the dryer for about five minutes before I hang it outside on the line. I don't understand the principle; I just know it works.

HIRING HELPERS

If the tasks you face still seem overwhelming, how about hiring some extra hands? "Oh no," you answer. "It's my job to do all the work. After all, I'm a fulltime house-keeper and mother." Or, "I am working because we need the money. I can't afford to hire outside help." To both responses I say, "A little help will go a long way and won't cost as much as you think."

I'm not talking about a housekeeper who costs any-where from $5 to $15 an hour. I'm talking about someone who wants to make some extra money. A teenager, maybe. Or an older woman who lives in your neighborhood or goes to your church or synagogue. Ask this person to cook for you two afternoons a week in your home or hers, making two dishes you can store and a hot meal for that night. Pay her a few dollars an hour if she's a teen, a little more if she's older, and ask her to follow your preplanned menus, using the food you already have in your kitchen.

The same principle will work for errands. Do you know a 16-year-old who just received a driver's license? What is the most important thing to him or her? Driving. Any-where, anytime. Give the teen your keys and let him run your errands. If you use your daybook shopping list, a teenager can do your grocery shopping for you. I wouldn't send an immature or irresponsible young person on such an assignment, but there are dependable teens in our neigh-borhood—and yours, too, I'm sure. It's also a nice way to reach out and help someone!

What about sending your ironing out? A woman who lives near me used to iron David's shirts for 45 cents each and my tablecloths for a dollar. When I get behind I've also been known to hire someone to do the heavy monthly jobs, like cleaning the refrigerator and the stove.

I am amazed that home delivery doesn't necessarily cost more, and is sometimes even less, than doing the shopping myself. The man who picks up and delivers my cleaning charges me 50 cents less than the local cleaner. I seldom even see him, since we have a prearranged spot where I leave the clothes to be cleaned or the check for the cleaned clothes, and he returns my finished cleaning. Many grocery stores have a delivery service for any area that is within walking distance for a store clerk.

STEP-SAVERS

Here are a few final step-saving, time-saving tips to help keep your household running smoothly:

+ Hang a message board in a central place in your house, like the kitchen, so family members can easily write a note when they leave on an errand. Ours is 23 years old. It was Anissa's childhood chalkboard. We use it at the front door for messages and to welcome our guests.

+ Instead of writing out your name, address, city, state, and zip code every time you address an envelope, have a stamp made with this information on it.

+ Keep a red pen or pencil at hand whenever you are reading a catalog, so you can note the items that interest you. Also, keep a pen, pencil, and paper in one of the drawers in your bathroom or on the back of the bathroom door so you can note when you run out of toiletries.

9

 **Win the Great Paper Chase**

*H*ow many of you have a pile of paper somewhere in your home? Two? More? Ninety-eight percent of all homes in America have at least one pile of paper. If you're like most people, there are piles on your kitchen counter, on the dining room table, on top of the refrigerator, under the bed, next to the bed, on the dresser, and on the desk. Rolltop desk sales are booming—they conceal the piles so easily! (No, I am not your neighbor and I have never seen your desk.)

What is in the pile? The contents in each home are surprisingly similar: school papers, receipts, catalogs, junk mail, flyers, newsletters that you want to read, letters, photographs, bills, important papers, and papers that need to be saved or at least located when you need them. The wedding invitation is in the pile, the bill is in the pile, the address for your husband's new boss is in the pile. It is safe and there is security in "the pile."

How many times have you been through the pile looking for something? A bill now past due. The wedding invitation you need within the hour to find the location of the church. The stack of photographs from Christmas that you want to show a friend who stopped in for coffee in April.

Periodically you attack the pile. One Saturday morning you declare war, promising yourself after discarding over 40 percent of the pile that this will never happen again. But it does—again and again.

I know, I did the same thing for years. While offering women tools to organize their planners, laundry rooms, children, closets, kitchens, and garages, I never covered the topic of paper.

Paper, paper, paper. I liked the looks of it, the feel of it, the ability to retrieve and reread originals. There were notes in my Aunt Pat's handwriting, letters from loved ones, greeting cards, magazine articles, and scraps of this and that. No matter what it was, I saved it. There was some order. The bills were filed. The warranties and guaranties had a home. The insurance and automobile papers were retrievable, but the rest sat in the corner of my desk piling higher and higher. Every system I had tried had failed. They were either too complicated or did not offer enough variety. In 1985 I made a commitment to the Lord and to myself that I would create a system that would work for me and that could be used to help other women. If it would work in our home, I was certain it would work anywhere.

The key concept was "File it, don't pile it." Two main facts surfaced. First, the pile represented work to be completed. I would need to file the records, send the check, RSVP the party, fill out the questionnaire for the school district, return the call. Second, most of the contents of the pile came directly through the mail. These facts formed the foundation of a plan that has worked in our home successfully. I hope you will try it. Be sure to adapt or modify whenever necessary. The relief from not having a pile on the corner of my desk has been a tremendous blessing. The time I have saved from searching through "the pile" again and again has been used more profitably.

This project requires work, but it also offers many rewards. There's the reward of knowing where everything is.

The reward of supplying the tax information when April 15 is around the corner. The reward of handing the original documents, plus receipt, for the refrigerator to the repairman so the $83 it cost to repair the icemaker is waived. The reward of sending your children off each morning with lunch forms, picture money, and signed report cards.

God is a God of order. He speaks to us about order. There is wisdom in order. Even keeping records for the generations to come is modeled for us in Scripture.

The Bible is a record. It's history—"His story." From Genesis, where the account of creation is given, to Revelation, where those who have been found faithful have their names written in the Book of Life, the Bible teaches us how important storing information is to God.

In it there are the genealogies that prove Jesus was of the line of David and so fulfills prophecy. There are life stories of individuals like Job, Ruth, Joseph, Paul, and Apollos, which inspire us to walk rightly before our Lord. There are amazingly detailed descriptions of how Noah was to build the ark and how Solomon was to build the temple. The Bible even describes where the cedar for the temple would be found, in Lebanon.

The amazing amount of detail and the order of the entire Bible encouraged me to believe that the pile on my desk is important to God, and that the records of the Otto family are important to the next generation. I genuinely hope that Scripture itself will be a constant reminder to you of the importance of order.

After returning from a 14-day holiday, I weighed the mail, not including newspapers or magazines. It weighed 21 pounds! It is true that we probably have more mail than the average family because of my speaking and writing, but not much.

The advent of the computer was hailed as the leap into a "paperless society." Not in our lifetime! The computer has certainly freed us from some aspects of paper, but from all accounts it has created significantly more paper rather than less.

By now I am confident you are saying, "Okay, you know my need. I'm ready, help me." As we have seen throughout this book, preparation is the key to organization. So before you tackle your "pile," be prepared. I have organized a list of tools you will need to accomplish your task easily and efficiently. You have most of these tools at home already. Gather them together and begin.

EQUIPMENT NEEDED

- ✦ 1 letter opener
- ✦ 1 red pen or highlighter
- ✦ 1 filing cabinet or storage box to hold family files
- ✦ 1 file sorter to hold minimum of 15 files
- ✦ 10-20 colored file folders
- ✦ 1 expandable file
- ✦ 2 medium to large baskets with or without handles
- ✦ 1 Rolodex or 3 x 5 file box with alphabetical tabs and 3 x 5 cards
- ✦ 1 large marking pen
- ✦ 1 file folder with inside pockets
- ✦ 1 stamp with your name and address
- ✦ 1 stamp pad
- ✦ 1 form letter
- ✦ 1 large trash can
- ✦ 12 envelopes marked January–December
- ✦ 12 folders marked January–December
- ✦ 1 pencil/pen cup holder
- ✦ 1 pad of paper at each phone
- ✦ 1 organizer/planner

Where does most of your paper come from? The mail. Your postal worker brings you a daily pile. I met a woman several years ago who approached me as I was finishing a class on organization. She spoke softly, as she did not want her friends to discover her dilemma. "Donna," she said, "I really need help in an area you did not cover today. You see, I am paralyzed by the mail. My husband has installed the largest mailbox the government will allow because I never take the mail out of the box, or at least not until it is so full that the postman comes to the door and says, 'Mrs. _____ you must take the mail out of the box.'" This dear woman had so many piles inside she didn't know what to do with the mail that kept coming. This is an extreme case, but I am learning not to be surprised by the stories I hear regarding confusion over the paper, records, and mail in homes.

A normal routine for handling the mail is to flip through each piece looking for the fun stuff—the personal letters, the envelopes with the Hallmark crest on the envelope, etc. You read those before you get in the door from the mailbox. The rest is *just* mail, and that is what ends up in your pile. It may be days or weeks before you slit open the rest of the mail. It may even take a telephone being disconnected before you realize the telephone bill is in the pile, unpaid.

It is necessary to move from piling to filing. That does not mean you will do the *work* of the mail, paying the bills, responding to the letters, or RSVPing as you open the mail. What it does mean is that you will process the mail, sort the mail, and file the mail instead of piling it. It also means you'll be able to find whatever you need whenever you want it. Remember, what makes you tired is not what you do, but what you don't do. The undone projects that hang over our shoulders wear us out.

THE MOST ESSENTIAL TOOL—DISCIPLINE

If you are ever going to get a handle on the paper in your

home, the first step you must accomplish every time you sort the mail is this:

DO NOT OPEN ONE PIECE OF MAIL UNTIL
YOU MAKE TIME TO OPEN IT ALL!

This is your single most important task, and you must train yourself to do it. Even if there was a letter from our daughter, if I didn't have time to slit all the mail, sort it, and file it, I did not open any of it. It worked! For the first time in years, I had control of the paper at my desk. The longest I could leave a special piece of correspondence was three days. At the end of three days I made time to sort and file the mail. Try it. You will be so pleased with your progress.

A STEP-BY-STEP APPROACH

You have your equipment and your discipline. You are ready. Each piece of equipment is used in the sorting and filing.

What comes in your mail? Letters, bills, newsletters, junk mail, catalogs, magazines, personal correspondence, invitations, mail for other family members, and solicitations. In every case, you need to follow the same process. Slit the envelope, underscore important information and file in the appropriate container. Let's go through each piece of equipment and its purpose.

Letter Opener—Slit all the envelopes open before you start sorting (turn the envelopes upside down and slit each one).

Red Pen or Highlighter—As you begin to empty each envelope, have your red pen handy for underscoring any items that need attention or need to be referred to later.

Filing Cabinet or Storage Box—This will hold family files and records that you need, but which you do not need or use every day.

File Sorter—This holds "working files"—files you use every time you open the mail. (These files are listed and described later in this chapter.)

Colored File Folders—I encourage the use of colored file folders because people remember the color of the file folder long after they forget how they labeled the file.

For years I had all of my photos and press releases in a blue file folder. It became ragged on the edges. I made a new file. The next time I needed a press release, I went to the right area looking for my blue file...I looked and looked. Just when I was ready to give up, I remembered I had made the new file. It was in the right place, but it was yellow, and I wasn't looking for yellow! Color also helps you find a file easier if it does become misplaced.

Your working files are essential in this process of moving mountains of paper. So let's spend a few minutes talking about them more specifically. The following list of file names will give you some ideas for what you'll want to create in your home.

Finances—If you don't pay the bills as they come, slit your envelope, check for mistakes, and drop into your file marked FINANCES.

Phone—If there is a mistake on your telephone bill, underscore it with your red pen and drop it into your phoning file. The invitation to the baby shower needs an RSVP—place it in the phoning file. (Try your best to RSVP all of your invitations promptly. My rule of thumb is call within 24 hours of receipt of the invitation. If you have ever tried to plan a party not knowing how many people will need a chair to sit on or food to eat, you know how frustrating it is not to receive RSVPs). When you make one phone call, you can make them all at the same time.

January–December—Have one file for each month of the year. Drop the wedding invitation for June into the file marked JUNE. Drop the plane tickets for the summer vacation, plus the hotel reservation, into the file marked JULY. Find a home for the dentist appointment before school begins in the AUGUST file. Get the idea?

Personal Correspondence—This file holds all the letters I receive that I am going to answer. Usually I read a letter from a friend and want to sit right down and respond. However, I most often do not. Instead, I underscore parts of the letter I want to respond to as I read it the first time. This makes it easier to answer at a later date.

Files for Family Members—Make one for your husband, each child, or anyone else you may be responsible for. Currently, my 88-year-old father-in-law lives with us. Daily I receive information for him about his health, finances, banking, and so on. I have a file marked DAD OTTO; all the material is secure in this file. The children's school activities, calendars, summer plans, ideas, and miscellaneous information will be easily found if you file it in their individual files.

To File—Say you have paid your insurance bill, and they send you the policy or binder. It needs to be filed in your filing cabinet, but not right now. You are just sorting and filing the daily mail now. This piece of mail can be filed later.

To Do—Follow the same principle as TO FILE. These are miscellaneous items that you must do or one-time events or items that do not need a special folder but will require work.

Coupons—If you take your coupon cutting and collecting seriously, you no doubt have a working system. But if you are like me, collecting a few each week, a file folder in your sorter is a great place to drop coupons cut from the Sunday newspaper.

Articles—Most of us have a favorite topic or hobby, something we are interested in. It may be golf or home design, or anything else. When I began teaching women about home organization, I had one file titled HOME HELPS. Today I have a full drawer of files, one for every room in the house. May I recommend you create a file that will store your articles and information on your favorite topics?

Hot—There are certain times when I have projects that include activities that must be done each day: calls, tallying of guests, or responses to requests. These are "musts." During these peak times, I put a red file folder in the center of my desk marked HOT, so I know these items have to be done "today."

Expandable File Folder—This is truly my favorite suggestion. In our mail we get "newsletters," "mini-magazines," and "updates" from favorite people and organizations. I want to read them all. Again, I don't usually have time when I am sorting the mail. Before I learned to "file it not pile it," I would think, "I wish I had some of those newsletters to read," as I was running out the door to a doctor's appointment, ball game, or plane ride. Now when I sort the mail, I drop all of this material into my expandable file folder marked READING. As I get ready to go, I simply grab my file from the file sorter. No more 1977 *National Geographic* for me.

Two Medium or Large Baskets—The mail brings many magazines and catalogs. Usually these are pile builders. Use one of your two baskets for catalogs and one for magazines. When a new catalog comes, discard the old copy and replace it with the new edition. There are times when you will not use your catalog for several months, but when you need it, you'll know where it is. Keep your magazine basket close to your reading chair.

Rolodex or 3 x 5 File with Alphabetical Tabs—Women truly enjoy personal telephone books. The pretty designs on the cover entice us; the white pages beckon us to fill them to the brim. We are drawn to them in stationery departments. Sometimes we even buy a pen to match. Having transferred all that information, what happens next? In a few months, the pen dries up, the book corners become creased, and because there isn't a scrap of paper for the pizza order handy, we have to write it on the telephone book...and on and on it goes. In five years we are ready to invest in a new book.

In place of this old-fashioned system, I suggest a Rolodex or 3 x 5 box system. Both work on the same principle: one card per family or person. When an individual moves, tear up the card and make a new one. Some of my cards are more than 30 years old (aunts and uncles who live in Chicago and haven't moved since I graduated from high school). In addition, your card can record Christmas card information, weddings, or birth announcements.

Marking Pen—Use this to make labels on your file folders.

File Folder with Inside Pockets—Prepare this file with stationery, notes, envelopes, pen, stickers, postcards, and postage stamps, and whatever else you normally use to write letters. Store this file folder in your sorter. Handle it like your reading file. If you know you are going to have to wait somewhere, take this file and your personal correspondence file and answer your letters. Recently, I had to get a title for a car. I read the entire reading file and answered five letters while I waited.

In the past, all of that material would have been sitting in the pile at home.

Stamp and Stamp Pad—Have a rubber stamp made with your name, address, city, state, and zip. It will save you time every time you pay bills or send mail. (This also makes a great gift idea for under $5!)

Form Letter—The junk mail keeps coming, rain or sun. Don't let it eat up your time, Instead, send a form letter. Here is an example.

> Dear ____
>
> Please remove my name from your mailing list. I do not wish to receive any further information, publication, or catalog from your organization. Thank you for giving this matter your earliest attention.
>
> Sincerely,
>
> Donna Otto

I had 50 of these made in a 5 x 7 size. Over a six-month period I recorded the results. Approximately 80 percent of those who received this letter pulled me from their mailing lists. Remember, you will find a self-addressed envelope in most of this junk mail. Sometimes it is even postage paid. Use it. Send your prepared form letter in their envelope and look forward to less junk mail daily.

Large Trash Can—It's obvious, but the operative word is *large*. Did you know you discard in direct proportion to the size of your trash can? You do. So get a big one. Remember back to the days of "the pile." When you finally declared war on the pile, over 40 percent was discarded.

Twelve Envelopes with January–December on the Front—This is the simplest and easiest way to be prepared for April 15. Just drop your receipts in the current month's envelope. By the end of the year you have already sorted everything by month. If time permits, write on the receipt what it represents, but if not, you can usually piece it together in April.

Pen and Pencil Holder—Use a cup or jar or cute container, one that will hold more than one pen or pencil. My mother was often heard saying, "That pen must have had legs so it could just get up and walk away." You know how frequently pens and pencils disappear, so be prepared.

Pad and Pencil at Each Phone—For the messages, of course!

Organizer/Planner—Discussed earlier.

This "file it, don't pile it" approach can be done in one full swoop or accomplished in sections. The most important step will be to discipline yourself not to open any of the mail until you can open and sort all of it. If you will follow these directions, the mail opening and sorting will be handled in five to eight minutes per day.

Some of you are saying, "You haven't seen my piles." For the truly avant-garde individual, I suggest going to the pile and pitching the entire thing. Except for photos and personal correspondence, it is all replaceable. They will send you another bill, bank statement, insurance policy, or calendar from school. The newsletters will arrive every 30 days, magazines weekly, and junk mail daily. The one-step method will give you immediate freedom, and you can begin your new "file it, don't pile it" with tomorrow's mail.

I recognize that would not be comfortable for the majority, but if it fits for you, try it!

I warned you this project would require work. Is writing a letter worth it? Does anyone care? Is saving, storing, and recording family records important? During World War II, Ed Burgess wrote love letters home to his young bride who was pregnant with their first child. Fifty-five years later, that child, having buried both of her parents within 18 months, found the carefully stored and saved letters. They were a tangible reminder of the love her parents had for each other and for her. They are a treasure she will guard for the next generation. Be orderly. Use wisdom in saving family records. There is great reward in it.

10

Free Your Life of Wardrobe Woes

I *don't agree with the old saying, "The clothes make the woman," but I do like to look my best. Clothes* are an important part of that, but having a nice wardrobe does not require the money most women think it does. The secret is in buying the proper clothes and then using them to the best advantage.

Wardrobe Activity Wheel

I recommend that every woman begin by finding out what kinds of clothes she needs the most. I suggest that you make a wardrobe activity wheel (Form 44 at the end of this chapter). Think about how you spend your time. Do you go to an office every day, so that you wear heels and a suit or a skirt and shirt? Do you spend 40 or 50 hours of your week in that kind of clothing? If so, then you're going to mark out the majority of your wheel for work clothes.

Are you a mom who has four small children at home? Do you spend the majority of your week in jeans and a T-shirt or slacks and a shirt? If so, then the majority of your wheel will be allotted to leisure wear.

In similar fashion, make sections for the time spent

in aerobics class (leotards), playing tennis (shorts, tops, tennis shoes), attending church (dresses, suits), and other activities. Once you have your activity wheel filled in, you'll know what type clothes you want in your wardrobe.

I began to build a wardrobe 25 years ago. Back then I wore dress clothes more often than I wore casual clothes, just as I do now. So I bought a good black suit, since black was one of my best colors. I had black shoes and a black bag so I didn't have to worry about buying accessories.

The next skirt I bought was a black-and-white tweed that I could wear with the jacket to my black suit. Next I bought a wine colored shirt, which could be worn with my black suit and also with my tweed skirt and the black suit jacket.

Eventually, I bought a gray suit. This purchase increased my mixing and matching possibilities. I could wear the gray suit jacket with my black skirt and the black suit jacket with the gray skirt. I could also wear the gray jacket with my black-and-white tweed skirt. Each outfit could be completed by the white, wine, and black shirts I owned. I began with a white silk shirt, added the wine silk shirt, followed by a different style white silk, because my activity wheel indicates my demand for dressy shirts. After I secured four or five dressy shirts, I purchased a white Oxford. And so it continued right down to today. I still have a diverse wardrobe of styles and fashions, still based on the original black and white.

Women sometimes say to me, "Oh, I don't wear a suit. I don't need a blazer. I don't need a jacket."

I reply, "If you wear sweaters or jackets of any kind, a suit jacket will be just as acceptable as that sweater or jacket, and oftentimes it will look nicer. So I would encourage you to consider a suit, maybe even a three-piece suit if you wear slacks."

COLOR ANALYSIS

Before you select the base color for your wardrobe, I recommend that you do a color analysis of yourself, or have someone else do it. If you do not know the color harmonies, hues, and shades that are most flattering to your skin tone, eye color, and hair, I suggest you begin by reading the book *Color, the Essence of You* by Suzanne.

Suzanne, a woman now in her late seventies, lives in San Francisco where she has spent 30 years counseling and dealing with color and its effect on people. "The effect of color on human beings," she says, "and on their lives is a vital, dynamic force which cannot be ignored." I agree with her.

Suzanne developed a color analysis system based on the four seasons of the year, which display natural arrays of color. She studied these, recorded and charted them, and then showed women how to relate these seasonal colors to their skin tones. All women have one of two undertones to their skin: either a blue, cool tone or a golden, warm tone. Let me briefly summarize the key elements of each season for you.

Spring colors are fresh and have a full intensity: the bright colors of tulips, the yellow of the crocus, and the green of new grass. Women who look good in spring colors have a golden tone to their skin.

Summer colors are the soft, hazy tones of the warm months. A summer person has a blue tone to her skin. She looks best in soft white, lavenders, mauves, beige and browns that have a hint of rose, and most blues, except royal blue, chinese blue, and dark navy.

Autumn colors are the flaming oranges, brilliant reds, and bold yellows of the changing leaves and the rich earth tones. Women who wear these colors have a warm, golden tone to their skins.

Winter colors reflect the drama and high contrast of a sparkling winter landscape. The best colors for a winter person are clear with sharp contrasts, true blue, hot turquoise, royal purple, and pure white and black, which I selected for my base wardrobe colors. I am a winter person. My hair is very dark, and I have dark eyes. I have a blue base to my skin. I have always known black and white looked good on me.

You will also have already made some wise color decisions. However, when you get ready to clean out your closet after you have been color analyzed, you'll find that the garments you haven't worn will often be colors that are not in your color palette. Don't think that you should throw away garments if they are still in good condition. Instead, you will want to find a scarf or accessory that harmonizes with that dress or suit and is also in your color palette.

CLOSET REALIGNMENT

Always carry your color palette with you. Most analysts provide these palettes with their color analyses. Whenever you are shopping, use these swatches to keep your purchases in tandem with the rest of your color-coordinated wardrobe.

Most women shop in exactly the opposite way and, as a result, they spend far more money than they should, and they keep their closets cluttered with impulse purchases. For example, I was recently browsing in a boutique when I heard a woman say, "Oh, I've just got to have this green suit; I don't have anything green in my wardrobe." When I heard that, several things occurred to me.

First, I wondered if she knew what colors she should wear to best enhance her appearance. Second, I wondered how long it would be before that woman realized that an $82 dress would actually run her $150 by the time she also purchased a handbag, shoes, belt, and other accessories to match it. And, finally, I wondered if she would have room in her closet for yet another random purchase.

Ironically, this is the very sort of woman who will attend one of my seminars and say, "I can't understand why my bedroom closet is always a mess."

Well, to eliminate your closet mess, begin to discard items along these lines:

◆ What clothes are you holding onto for strictly sentimental reasons?

More than 25 percent of your wardrobe hangs there out of sentiment and takes up needed space even though it's never worn. Get rid of that stuff. Now!

You haven't worn your high school cheerleading outfit for 20 years. The skirt is too long, the colors are faded, and there's a moth hole in the sleeve Besides, you've had children since then and you now have a different shape Save your picture of the old squad, but get rid of the outfit or save it in your storage system in a memorabrlia or costume box.

A miniskirt you wore to the sorority dance as a college freshman? The paisley ski pants you wore on the vacation to Vail? The balloon-sleeve blouse you bought on impulse in the Bahamas? Yank those things out of there and give them away, throw them away, or haul them off to the attic for costumes. Focus on retaining those items of clothing that serve the current you.

Am I suggesting that you pitch your wedding dress or your husband's old military uniform? Of course not. We all have certain items of clothing that represent treasured times in our lives. They must be saved. In fact, these clothes should be dry-cleaned, mothproofed, and stored in your storage system. I believe that any item of clothing that hangs in your closet for a season without being worn should be discarded, unless you have some special use planned for it.

Remember that 20-year class reunion party of my husband's? Well, one lady came dressed in a nice, but not fancy, cotton dress. Someone commented about her somewhat casual appearance at such a formal affair. She grinned self-confidently and then delivered a punchline I'll never forget: "It's the dress I wore the day we all graduated. After all these years, I'm still able to wear it."

> ✦ What things do you have that are not in your size?

We all like to think we will soon return to the smaller size we once were, but the truth of the matter is the odds are against us. It's usually best to admit this and give away clothes that no longer fit you or are too tight.

> ✦ Which items are out of vogue forever?

> ✦ Which pieces do I have needless duplicates and triplicates of that I can give to someone else?

> ✦ What do I have hanging there that I've borrowed from my sister or a friend and need to return?

Once you eliminate items according to these criteria, you already have plenty of "new room" in your closet. If not, then make use of your box storage system. If it is winter, neatly fold your spring and summer items into a box and fill out a 3 x 5 index card listing the box's contents. Store the box and leave your winter clothes in your bedroom closet.

Now put the retained clothes back in the closet in a way that will give them better use. Put all your jackets together, whether they are sport jackets, suit jackets, or dress jackets. Put all your slacks together too, and all your blouses and shirts and skirts.

Most women hang a suit on one hanger. Then they always wear that jacket with that skirt, instead of matching the suit jacket to other skirts. If you put on a dress that needs a light wrap and you have your jackets together, you might just find a suit jacket to go over your dress.

Now further organize your clothes by putting them together by color. Put all your blue shirts together, all of your white shirts together. I have a number of white shirts: a dressy, sheer blouse; a very severely tailored shirt; and some Oxford sport shirts. These shirts coordinate with most of my jackets and skirts.

If you wear hats, take one of your storage boxes and cover it with adhesive-backed vinyl paper or fabric. Use it to hold hats in your closet. Large sweater storage boxes also work effectively to hold scarves, belts, and other accessories. If you have a walk-in closet, as I do, you can use clear plastic containers set on built-in wooden shelves. Handbags can also be lined up on shelves.

If you begin to feel proud of your newly organized closet, enhance it even more. Cover the shelves with paper and repaint the walls. Then, when company comes, you can think up an excuse to open your closet and be pleased by the decorated interior.

COORDINATING PURSES

A cluttered and disorganized purse is one of the greatest frustrations of a woman's life. Don't you agree? How often do you rummage through a large purse to try to find a pen or house key or driver's license? Or carry a huge handbag when you go out for a nice dinner with your husband because you don't have time to change your purse? There are ways to control this. I can show you how to change that large purse into a smaller one in 30 seconds or less.

First, you must get prepared. Buy, or, if you are a seamstress, make, a variety of minipurses, or purse "pouches" as I call them. You must also have a good wallet that contains areas for the following items: coins, identification, checks and checkbook, pen, and credit cards. A useful wallet will hold everything you need to make purchases, so you will not have to dig to the bottom of your purse for pennies, pens, or your checkbook. You'll never hold up another check-out line at the grocery store if you have the proper wallet.

What goes into those pouches I mentioned? Lots of things. How many do I need? The sky is the limit. I have two pouches just for my cosmetics. One holds a tube of lipstick and a mirror. The second holds a bit more: perfume, eye makeup, mascara, an eyebrow brush, and an eyelash curler.

Another pouch could be called my "paper pouch," since it holds my color palette, envelopes that contain Christmas money for instant purchases (more about this later), and parking stubs. Still another pouch is my food pouch, which holds throat lozenges, toothpicks, sugarless candy and gum, artificial sweetener, raw sugar, and salt. A fifth pouch holds miscellaneous items: a sewing kit, nail file and clippers, a collapsible cup, a portable toothbrush, and toothpaste. I also have a pouch for reading glasses and a pouch for sunglasses.

You may substitute some of mine for ones that fit your particular needs, but by now you understand the principle: Organize related things together in pouches so you aren't always looking for small items.

Let's go back to that last-minute dinner invitation from your husband or boyfriend. When David says, "Let's go out to dinner," I quickly change my clothes, if necessary, and then grab a clutch bag and my everyday purse. Do I need my wallet? No, he's paying for dinner. Do I need my large cosmetic bag? No. But I do need the one with a tube of lipstick and a mirror. I grab this pouch from my everyday purse and put it in the clutch bag. In about 30 seconds I've selected the pouches I need. *Voilà!* I'm ready to go—before David has changed his mind. When I return home, I simply return these purse pouches to my everyday bag and, once again, I am prepared for tomorrow. Such simple steps give me confidence and freedom from worry that so often spoils our fun.

WARDROBE ACTIVITY WHEEL

Work, Sunday
dress clothes
(suits, dresses, dressy
shirts, heels)

Tennis Backpacking Shopping Lunches Casual Gardening Housecleaning

Wardrobe Inventory

Blouses _____   Dresses _____   Jackets _____
_____   _____   _____
_____   _____   _____
Shirts _____   _____   _____
_____   _____   _____
_____   Slacks _____   Sweaters _____
_____   _____   _____
Skirts _____   _____   _____
_____   _____   _____
_____   _____   _____
_____   _____   Accessories _____
Suits _____   Shoes _____   _____
_____   _____   _____
_____   _____   _____
_____   _____   _____
_____   _____   _____

11

Kids Can Help!

I *t's odd the way parental influence affects children.*
Even psychologists who have spent many years
studying child behavior patterns will admit that no one can
predict with accuracy how a child will turn out.

There once were identical twin boys who had a father
who was an abrasive and irresponsible alcoholic. When the
boys grew up, one wound up an alcoholic derelict and the
other was a teetotaler who was a successful executive.

A reporter interviewed the twins. When asked why he
turned out as he had, the alcoholic brother said, "With a
father like mine, what else could you expect?" When asked
why he turned out as he had, the teetotaler brother said,
"With a father like mine, what else could you expect?"

Children, just as adults, have free will. It's true that they
can be stubborn, rebellious, aggravating, and arrogant at
times. But so can adults. In truth, all children desire love
and approval from their parents. They take their relational
cues from parents and respond accordingly. "Like father,
like son" is more than just a cliché. Children imitate their
parental role models, and that's why it is never too early to
set good organizational examples for them.

My Uncle Jerry used to tell my cousin Joe, "If you want
to know what your girlfriend will be like in 25 years, look at

her mother now." Twenty-five years ago I used to scoff at that. But I don't anymore. I've since learned that things instilled early in children linger for many years.

So let's look at some organizational procedures that you can instill in your children, which will assist you now and them in the future.

TEACHING RESPONSIBILITY

In other countries, such as India, Thailand, and Singapore, six-year-old children are expected to help with the shopping and marketing. They carry the basket, take the food to the scales, weigh the food, and take charge of the younger children. They see themselves as shopping with their mothers rather than being taken along on a shopping trip. In the pioneer days of our own country, children, because of necessity, shared in the work. Individual tasks were thought to develop a child's character, and they were also unavoidable in households where every hand was needed just for survival. This old philosophy is as true for modern families as it was for our ancestors.

I know quite a few women like Jeffrey's mother, Jill, who works fulltime and feels overworked and harassed. The burden of cooking and housekeeping falls totally on her, despite a supportive husband, Bob, who helps with household repairs and sometimes does the shopping. Jill never considers the possibility of increasing little Jeffrey's responsibility. "It doesn't seem fair," she says, "to deprive him of his after-school time. I think he needs the opportunity to relax and daydream, to just fiddle around." To me, that sounds like a woman who feels guilty about working instead of feeling, "The family is in this together, and work has to be done. Let's make the best of it." It wouldn't hurt little Jeffrey to be given some household responsibilities. Jill shouldn't be afraid to say, "I need help."

How often do mothers hear the words, "I'm bored"? In our house we heard it frequently, believe me. What are children telling us? Basically, that they need some adult direction and challenge.

Seize the opportunities to say, "Okay, let's do some work together." Most kids love to work with their parents. (After all, "big people's" work is important.) Often "I'm bored" is nothing more than a cry for attention, a way of saying, "Spend some time with me."

You will find that when your reaction to their complaint changes from being angry to suggesting a work activity together, one of two things will occur; either they will stop saying, "I'm bored!" or they will learn a new task. My daughter's attitude improved with every 15 minutes of hard work or exercise.

If you are in doubt as to what kind of work a child can handle at a certain age, talk to the parents and children in your circle of friends. See what is expected of these children and what they are actually doing. You can also consult books, like *The First Three Years of Life* by Dr. Burton L. White or *How to Parent* by Fitzhugh Dobson.

Never assign a child a task until he or she has already had some success at it. Let me give you an example.

I use a squeegee on my mirrors and windows because of the time it saves me. I felt my daughter should be able to take over this job, so I demonstrated the procedure to her quickly. "One swipe across the top, which ends in an angle. One swipe down. One more swipe down. Now, doesn't that look terrific!" I handed the squeegee to my adolescent child and left the room.

A few minutes later she came walking into the room where I was, annoyed with herself—and with me I might add. "I can't do it," she protested firmly.

"Of course you can," I responded positively.

"No, I can't," she persisted. On and on we argued.

I had not given her clear enough instructions on how to apply the pressure evenly to avoid smears. I also had not allowed her to practice a few times before I left the room. Children don't like failing any more than we do. It is our responsibility to show them how to do something well enough to assure success. I spent longer dealing with her negative attitude than the time it would have taken to watch her practice the task in the first place. Yes, we should always be giving our children new jobs and new responsibilities as they grow older, but only after we've taught them how to complete the job successfully.

PROVIDING OPTIONS

One of the ways to train a child to do a variety of tasks while also helping him or her to exercise some choice is to use a job jar. We do this at our house.

Simply write on slips of paper some household jobs your child is capable of accomplishing or which you'd like your child to learn, such as "Clear away dinner dishes" or "Sweep the driveway" or "Dust the furniture." Then say to your child, "Choose any ten jobs (or two or three, depending on the child's age) for this week, I'll do the others." This gives the child the freedom of selection and reduces your overall work load. And you'll never hear "You always make me do . . ." again.

You can also make a job wheel with a dozen jobs listed in a circle. The child then can spin the spinner one to three times each day. In this way there's some fun, and no two days of jobs are alike. Obviously, the number of jobs a child can handle varies with the time of the year. I assigned my daughter fewer household duties during the school year than in the summer vacation months.

Children are most bored in the summer, which is natural since so much of their lives are organized in the school months. Penny, a friend of mine, decided to alleviate her daughter's boredom by planning a camp just for her. The five-year-old was allowed to invite three friends (two more crashed) to the camp, which met three days a week for the entire month of June. Penny charged a minimum fee for her camp, which she jokingly named Camp Henny Penny, to cover expenses and a bright-red T-shirt. Trips to the zoo, theaters, the parks, and the swimming pool were planned for two of the three days.

The other day was for at-home activities, like art work and table games. One day Penny allowed the children to make chalk drawings on her concrete driveway. Another day the children all worked together to create a three-by-three foot collage from magazine pictures. Still another day they took pictures of each other with a Polaroid camera and pasted the pictures onto pieces of paper. Penny asked them to write the answer to the question, "What have I learned about my new friend?" below each child's picture.

Needless to say, Camp Henny Penny was a big success.

SCHOOL PAPERS AND DECISION MAKING

Although you'll never convince a child of it, not every piece of paper he or she brings home is valuable. Not every picture needs to be hung up or saved. Your whole house cannot become a gallery for his or her artwork. But how do you tell this to the budding artist? How do you throw some drawings away without dampening the child's artistic spirit? You simply allow your son or daughter to learn to make decisions in this area of his or her life.

The length of time an individual keeps the papers depends upon the age of the child. To a preschooler a week is an infinite amount of time. For a teenager you may encourage keeping schoolwork for a six-week or nine-week grading term and then discard those that will not be needed for a final exam or that have sentimental value. Once, our daughter received a C in a course at school and was ready to blame the teacher for the poor mark. After we sorted through her accumulated papers, we realized that, in fact, her average grade was a C. Having the papers allowed her to accept responsibility for the grade and to try harder during the next grading session (and she did improve!).

Keeping papers in a specified place for a limited time encourages the child to learn that clutter is not a good idea. An acrylic holder, inexpensive to buy, or a wall rack will hold a week's worth of papers and also make the child feel important. At the end of the week say, "All right, Nathan, since we can't keep all these papers, please select this week's best paper. We'll save one a week in this file." In the beginning they may protest or find making the decision difficult. Allowing your son or daughter to select the ones to keep or discard teaches decision making. Taking the time to go through the papers occasionally provides an excellent opportunity to affirm your child's work and spend some special time together.

I kept a special folder of my daughter's artwork. At the end of the school year, she sorted through the selection and chose the best ten to save as representative of her work for that year. (If your child finds it hard to throw away certain favorite papers, you can suggest, "Let's send this one to Grandma to show her how well you are doing in school.")

KEEPING TRACK OF BELONGINGS

I have devised a method of keeping track of children's belongings after many mornings of searching frantically for a math book or a homework assignment. My system also eliminates the unexpected midmorning telephone call. "Mom, would you please bring my science book to school? I forgot my homework," admits the squeaky voice on the other end of the line.

Let me tell you what to do. Just inside each child's bedroom, set a basket, milk carton crate, box, or shopping bag on the floor. If your children share a room, you will need two baskets. Each child must have his own.

Once Susie finishes her homework, have her put her assignments into the appropriate textbooks, and then place all the books into the basket. If Susie has to take picture money or field trip money, put the forms, the money, and the permission slip into an envelope and place the envelope in the basket. If she needs lunch money, into the basket it goes. Add her gym clothes for the next day, gym shoes, and anything she wants to take for show-and-tell. Lastly, let her add her clothes for the next morning, checking to see that her socks and belt are there (Illustration 8). Even a preschooler who has a nursery school or ballet classes can do this. It helps a child develop organizational habits early in life.

Illustration 8

USING MONEY AND TIME

It's a good idea to pay your children to do some of the

jobs you might normally hire nonfamily members to do. Teenagers can paint rooms, cut the grass, wash and wax the car, weed the garden, and run errands. Then, if they ask you for snack money, date money, or video game money, you can remind them they have their own funds to use.

One man raised his son by giving him a set allowance each week for completion of a list of duties. The father only paid out half the allowance, however. He made the son save the other half in a piggy bank until the amount reached $15. Then the boy could spend it all at once.

Over the years the father regularly increased the list of duties and the amount of the allowance, but he held to the rule of "spend half, save half." As the boy, time and again, saw the power of accumulated money, he willingly stayed in the habit of saving. Years later, when he was in high school, the boy bought himself a set of drums, a computer, and a second-hand car because he had learned how to save and manage money.

And just as teenagers can be taught how to manage money, they also can be taught how to manage time. You may want to give your teenager a daybook. At first some of the kids laughed at my daughter carrying her daybook around, just as my classmates had laughed at me. Still she persisted. She came to realize that she was able to get more done than many of her classmates by using the planner.

Her daybook was not as thick as mine. She had a month-at-a-glance section in which she scheduled her social activities, her church activities, and her babysitting jobs. Then, instead of today pages, she used week-at-a-glance forms, two pages facing each other, with spaces for each day of the week. She used additional dividers and pages to assist her with special projects, plus a telephone directory and a zippered bag. A daybook makes a great graduation gift for high school and college seniors.

YOUNG CHILD SAFETY

Do all you can to insure your child's safety while also reducing your work load. For example, if you buy your young child shoes with Velcro flaps, the child won't trip over dangling shoelaces nor ask you to tie his shoes.

Don't buy 100 percent cotton clothing for children. Avoid anything that has to be ironed. Make sure that you buy clothes that fasten in the front. Sew buttons on with elastic thread, which stretches and makes the button go through the buttonholes more easily. In winter use sleeve clip-ons for mitten holders and buy boots that slip on easily rather than needing to be buckled, or attach metal rings to boot zippers to make them easier to pull.

COMING AND GOING

If you take your children for a visit to a friend's home, try to prepare them for your departure. Don't simply announce, "Come on. Time to leave!" Instead, give the child a ten-minute warning, such as, "You need to start helping Kent pick up the playroom, Jason. We need to get going in about ten minutes." This shows the child that you know she has been involved in something important too, and that you want her to have adequate time to draw it to a conclusion. At our house we rang a bell five minutes before meals, departure times, and scheduled work activities.

LAUNDRY DETAIL

Sorting the laundry can become a game for younger children. Pile all the dirty clothes on the floor of your laundry room. Get three big bags—laundry bags or king-size pillow cases or drawstring bags you make yourself—one colored, one dark, and one white. Gather the children around.

Pick up a pair of your husband's jeans. "These are Daddy's dark jeans. They go in this dark bag. These are your brightly colored shorts. We put them in this brightly colored bag. These are your white socks. They go in this white bag." You might want to mark each bag with a swatch of the proper color or with the words *dark clothes, white clothes, colored clothes* if your children are older.

"Now let's see you do it. John, where should we put your dirty pair of jeans?" The game goes on and on until you see a glimmer of understanding in the children's eyes. Actually, most children age two and above catch on quickly once they learn their colors.

Once you train your children in good organizational habits, you'll discover more free time for fun activities you can enjoy together.

12

The Best Christmas Ever

A *woman who attended my Christmas seminars
said to me before the first session, "Did you ever*
hear the song, "The 12 Days of Christmas"? Can you imagine 12 days of Christmas? One day's bad enough." Maybe
you agree with her. Maybe the Ziggy card I received one
Christmas describes how you feel perfectly.

Ziggy writes to a friend, "Holidays drive me crazy. Last
year I hung my Easter basket from the mantel with care,
stuffed my Christmas tree, put colored lights and tinsel on
my Thanksgiving turkey, and sent a shamrock to my valentine on Flag Day. But, as you can see, that still hasn't prevented me from wishing you a Merry Halloween."

Good ol' Ziggy—always closer to the truth than fiction.
Surely if there's anything that can throw a household into
an uproar, knock a budget out of kilter, and drive sane
people to maniacal behavior, it's a holiday. And particularly Christmas.

That's why in this chapter I am going to show you ways
to change your harried and hassled Christmastime into a
fun, fulfilling, and holy holiday. Let's begin by reminding
ourselves of what Christmas is supposed to be all about—
as opposed to what the merchants try to convince us it's all
about.

Capturing the Christmas Spirit

Before you begin to worry about what cookies you'll need to make or how tall a tree you should buy, try to decide what activities would make your Christmas truly meaningful. For us the memories of the meaningful experiences linger for years, but the fun often slips out of our minds before the next Christmas season. Think about how you can enrich your family life, spiritual life, and friendships. Here are some ideas to consider:

Share your prosperity. Find a family who is unable to reciprocate in your church or neighborhood and invite them to dinner one night, as Christ suggested in Luke 14:12-14. Another idea is to have each member of your family prepare one part of a meal—Dad can make a salad, Mom can prepare a covered main dish, Lisa can fix some rolls, and Joe can make pudding—and then everyone can take it to the home of a needy, retired, or shut-in family. Still another idea is to help serve a Christmas dinner with the Salvation Army or any local organization that traditionally serves a meal on Christmas day.

A highlight of my Christmas season is a traditional party given by a group of women in our church for the elderly residents of a local nursing home. Instead of taking the potluck dinner to the nursing home, the Epleys, a family in our church, host the party in their home. Some of the residents had not left the nursing home in ten years prior to our first party. Now we enjoy a festive dinner together, sing songs, and share with each other what Christmas means to us. Then we give each guest a gift.

As these people leave the party, I have heard remarks like, "This is truly one of the best Christmases I've had in a long time." One man told me his wife was afraid to go out, but she came to our party because her friends had told her how much fun they had had the year before. The director of the nursing home told us that early in November the women come to her and ask, "What shall I wear for the big Christmas celebration at the Epleys' home?" One elderly woman got dressed and went down to the foyer to wait for her ride two days in advance because, in her excitement, she had forgotten the actual date.

Read Christmas books. To help you focus on the meaning of this holiday, go to the library and get an armload of seasonal classics and spend time each day reading aloud to your children and sharing Christmas readings as a family. Charles Dickens's *A Christmas Carol*; George MacDonald's *The Christmas Stories of George MacDonald* (published by David C. Cook, Elgin, Illinois); Luci Shaw's book, *The Sighting of the Green*, especially the poem, "Mary's Song"; Dylan Thomas's *A Child's Christmas in Wales*; and Jack London's short story, "A Klondike Christmas" are just a few of the many literary classics. Don't forget *A Cup of Christmas Tea* by Tom Hegg, *The Gift of the Magi* by O. Henry, and *Santa, Are You for Real?* by Harold Myra.

Our family enjoys reading *The Best Christmas Pageant Ever* by Barbara Robinson. A few years ago my sister-in-law and her family spent the first Christmas after the death of her husband with us. As usual, we read this story. Guess who enjoyed it most? My 17-year-old nephew Tom, a six-foot-three, 240-pound linebacker.

Play Christmas music. Put on your favorite holiday tunes and let them play as you dust, wash dishes, play a game with the family, or decorate the tree. Better yet, get some songsheets and gather everyone around the piano and have a sing-along one night. Let the small children have solo parts on "Away in the Manger" and "We Three Kings," and then get everyone involved in a long-winded version of "The 12 Days of Christmas."

Save your Christmas cards. Put them in a basket or container. We put ours in a napkin holder. Every day of the next year, starting on January 1, we take one of those Christmas cards out and pray for that person or family at dinnertime. Then I staple the Christmas card together, and on the backside of the card, where it's white, I draw a line down the middle and make it into a postcard. I write the name and address of the person who sent the card and stamp it. On the left side of the card I just write a note saying, "Hi: Today is June 12, and we prayed for you this morning. Trust you are having a good year."

Have a birthday party for Jesus. Make a cake, invite some neighborhood children, sing "Happy Birthday" to Jesus, play pin-the-tail-on-Mary's-donkey, eat raisins, dates, and cookies, and celebrate His birthday. Or set a place for Jesus on Christmas morning. You might want to use a special Christmas plate.

Plan family caroling parties. Select four or five special Christmas songs and practice them as a family. Then go to the door of some friend's house and start singing. When they invite you in, say, "No. Not until you you've heard our full repertoire." It'll be a time of laughs and good cheer.

"Oh, but Donna, you haven't heard me sing," you moan. "I'm terrible."

"Not any worse than I," I answer. In 1975 I was politely asked to either sing more softly or leave the church choir. I have a terrible voice and can't stay on key for longer than three or four notes. Thankfully Anissa and David have dandy voices. Together, you'd think we were a trio straight from the Met! The family's contribution is often much more pleasing than the singing of any individual member.

These six ideas are just a few of the dozens of ways you can make Christmas a very special season for your whole family. Start thinking now. I know you'll be able to come up with other ideas.

MAKING CHRISTMAS PLANS

Most people start to think about Christmas as soon as the stores begin to decorate, and that's often as early as October. Still we tend to procrastinate our serious Christmas planning until the day after Thanksgiving. That's way too late, although I do think it's important to spend time celebrating Thanksgiving.

The time to begin planning Christmas is on December 26. That's right: As soon as this Christmas ends, you should already begin to think about next Christmas.

Why? Well, for one thing, it's the best time to shop for all your holiday necessities. On the day after Christmas you can go to your area department stores and purchase Christmas cards, ornaments, lights, nativity scenes, Christmas albums, candles, and wrapping paper at more than a 50 percent discount. Not only does that save you time next year, it also allows you extra money to spend on gifts and holiday festivities. I realize not everyone is up for shopping the day after Christmas. However, as we begin to store our Christmas treasures, we prepare for next year's holiday season.

Storage

We discussed storage procedures earlier. The same system applies to Christmas materials. Get some of your standard-size boxes, put your Christmas items in them, and make a 3 x 5 card for each box that lists the specific contents of the box. I have 47 storage boxes at my home. All of my Christmas boxes are numbered 25, but each has a letter code too (25-A, 25-B, 25-C).

There are two ways to store your Christmas materials. One way is to group things by category, such as putting all the wreaths in one box and all the electrical lights in another.

Another way is to store items according to the rooms of your house. One box, for instance, might be for your dining room. It would contain the Christmas linens, the holiday candles, the garland for the chandelier, a tablepiece, and a wall wreath.

The time to repair items is just before packing them. Trim the wicks of candles; replace burned-out lights and carefully coil the strands; glue together any broken parts of your manger scene. This all saves time next year. Remember, the key word in organization is *preparation*.

Shopping

As you begin the new year, try to save a few dollars per week—if possible, any amount from $2 to $20—for Christmas. For years I saved $5 a week from my grocery money. I keep this money in my purse at all times so I can benefit from special sales. For instance, my mom wanted a down pillow because she has arthritis and the doctor recommended one They regularly sell for $45 or more. In March a local department store had a special sale: down pillows at $25. I had my Christmas money in my purse, so I was able to purchase one before the supply was sold out.

As the year continues, keep Christmas in mind. If stores have end-of-season sales, perhaps you can buy a sweater for a relative or friend at a discount rate and store it. Close-out sales and store liquidation sales are also good places to get bargains. As you buy gifts, you can gift wrap them and store them in large plastic garbage bags to keep them from getting dusty.

Complete your shopping by the end of October or the middle of November at the latest. Any gift you have to send overseas must be mailed during the first week of November so that you can get the inexpensive boat rate rather than first-class airmail rates.

Jobs that Last

November is also the time to polish your silver serving pieces, to mail your Christmas get-together invitations, and to start preparing food items such as ice rings, potato dishes, pies, and anything else that will preserve well in your freezer.

Don't wait until the last minute and whisper to your husband, "Do you think my brother Paul could sit beside Aunt Suzie this year?" Decide the seating arrangements ahead of time. I take an 8½ x 11 piece of paper and put 14 $x's$ around the edge, since our dining room table seats this number of people comfortably. Together David and I discuss who knows whom and who would enjoy being together. Often we separate family members so people will have an opportunity to visit with others.

Plan what you will wear. Why do that so early? Take it from someone who has suffered the consequences of a quick decision. About ten years ago I bought a dress with a wide, wide belt and long sleeves for Easter. I had guests for dinner that afternoon, and by the time the meal was over, I was really suffering. The belt had become a noose around my waist. The long sleeves made my warm kitchen feel as if it were 90 degrees.

Now I wear long, wrap-around apron skirts. I put them over a shirt I have worn to work or church, and I'm ready to entertain. I can also wear flats with these long skirts and shed my hose. I'm a much more cordial hostess when I'm comfortable.

In the final days before Christmas, you should take time to review everything. Are the place cards written yet for the big family dinner? Are all the gifts wrapped and under the tree? Did you forget anyone? Do the family members have cleaned and pressed clothes for all the church events and parties they will be attending? Has the chimney been cleaned out to make ready for Santa?

If so, then relax and enjoy things.

PREPARING CHRISTMAS CARDS

Here is my honest opinion: I think that mailing imprinted Christmas cards to our friends and loved ones is a waste of time and money. You pay for the stamp, you pay for the card, you pay for the envelope. And what do people get from you? They get a card with some stranger's words on it and a printing of your name at the bottom of the inside. I ask you, what is *personal* about something like that?

People don't want to receive the embossed letters of your name. They want to receive news and greetings in your handwriting. They want updates on your activities, pictures of your children, announcements of your plans for next year.

It is possible for you to give them just that. Here's how: 1) buy your cards right after Christmas at an inexpensive rate; 2) have return address stickers printed with your name and address or have the store imprint your return address (some stores offer in lieu of signature); 3) during a lull in the summer months, get out the envelopes to the Christmas cards and address them; 4) right after Thanksgiving, get out your cards, jot a note on each one, and sign them personally; 5) if you have prepared a Christmas letter to copy and send to friends, send one along with each card.

Now, you may say, "But what if my friends move between summer and Christmas?" Simple. You address one or two envelopes over again; but, meanwhile, the other 100 are still ready to mail. What a relief for you and what a joy to those you write to.

PLANNING YOUR HOME DECORATING

Whenever someone enters your home, the decorating instantly tells that person how you celebrate the season. Home decorations can establish moods, endorse beliefs, lift spirits, and welcome visitors. They are an important part of the overall success of your Christmas plans.

We always decorate early. Actually I'd begin decorating on November 1, but David insists on waiting until the day after Thanksgiving. He always kids me about how fast I can turn our house into a red-and-green wonderland. It takes me about two days to decorate the house, but it would take longer if I didn't commandeer the entire family. Everyone joins in the fun and hassle.

I wrap every door in our house, like a package, with wide plaid taffeta ribbon, which I buy from a floral supply house very inexpensively. I use that ribbon for four or five years in a row. After you've wrapped the door four or five times, it gets a little worn. But then I cut out the worn spots, and I put that ribbon on packages. I wrap every inside door: the bedroom doors, the hallway door, even the closet doors. I usually add some kind of decoration, such as a piece of holly or an ornament or some bells to the bow in the middle of the door.

Decorations do not have to cost you a lot of money if you remember to use things that are all around you, virtually free of charge. Pull some pine cones from the trees in your yard; gather up all the loose ribbon scraps on your sewing table.

Your hometown library will have a wide selection of craft books, which you can borrow in order to make home-made Christmas tree ornaments and room decorations. A few dollars spent on yarn, felt strips, and spray paint will provide several nights of activities.

Most of the materials used in homemade ornaments are common household items such as cardboard boxes, egg cartons, aluminum foil, rags, string, rubber bands, bottle caps, and disposable plastic containers. Find a box of crayons, a pair of scissors, a ruler, some tape, and you're in business. Not only will you save money by making your own ornaments and decorations, you will personalize your

Christmas tree and will make it something special to every member of your family.

Colorful plants and greenery will add a warm Christmas glow to your den, living room, or dining area. Buy your holly and evergreens right before Christmas; arrange them in water and keep them away from heat vents. Split the stems so they can absorb water. Your poinsettia, chrysanthemum, cyclamen, azalea, and Christmas cactus will need full sunlight, medium humidity, and moist soil to survive well, Move the plants to a basement or cool room (55° F) at night if possible. This prolongs blooming. Note: Once your Christmas pepper and Jerusalem cherry plants lose their bloom, you can retain them as green plants, but they seldom bloom again.

Consider using a wreath for double duty, one year on the front door, the next year as a table centerpiece with a fat candle in the middle of it. Or use cones and candles and garlands and pine boughs and ribbons and bows and flowers and holly. Lay these festive items in the middle of the table, and put candles in the center of the arrangement. Tie ribbons on the glass at each individual place or tie ribbons on your candleholders and put red and green candles in them. They make beautiful table decorations.

If you have a number of candleholders—maybe they're white or glass or brass or red or green and of varying heights—just put them all in the center of the table and tie ribbons on them, letting the ribbon trail from the candleholders. Put some red and green candles in them. They make beautiful table decorations.

Sometimes I core an apple and put a red or green votive candle inside to make an individual candleholder at each person's place. At Thanksgiving I take an orange, clean out the center, and put a votive candle in it. You can also put the candles in the center of your table in various fruits or vegetables.

I use so many candles at Christmastime, my husband laughingly calls me a pyromaniac. I have candles in every room, the bathrooms, the bedrooms, the living room, the dining room. I save candles from year to year, especially my large decorator candles, some of which are 10 to 12 years old. I buy votive candles and put them in the big decorator candles, once they've burned enough to have a scooped-out hole, to preseve them. Obviously the candles get dusty, so I rub them with nylon hosiery to clean them.

Don't be trapped into thinking that the only fabric you can use as a tablecloth is linen or cotton. Try seersucker, cotton, polyester, wool, a lace curtain, sheets, wrapping paper, even wallpaper.

One year I decorated our table as a gift box to celebrate a friend's December birthday. I used aluminum foil, but wrapping paper foil, fabric, or wallpaper will work just as well.

Take the paper and literally wrap your tabletop as you would a package, using tape to secure the paper underneath the table. Then take a ribbon and wrap it around the table as you would a package, horizontally and vertically, to make a big bow which becomes your centerpiece. (This idea is also great for an organization's Christmas luncheon because of cost efficiency.) Small decorated boxes on the center of the table add a special effect, as do Styrofoam squares wrapped like gifts and used as place cards. When the party is over, just unwrap the table and throw the paper into the trash can.

It's also easy to make decorator napkin rings. Use toilet paper rolls or paper towel rolls and cut them into pieces. Nobody will ever know. Then put lace or ribbon around them. Paint and decorate clothespins and use those for napkin holders. Red or green plastic cookie cutters or aluminum cookie cutters also make wonderful napkin holders. Or you can just take Christmas ribbon and tie a napkin up and lay that on the plate. It looks pretty. Or cut a piece of green felt into a holly or wreath pattern for a napkin ring.

If you like to sew, make some felt stockings or Christmas boots. You can either make them big enough so you can put silverware and napkins inside or make them small enough just for your napkin. One final idea: Hold a napkin at two opposite ends and twist it as you would twist a wet towel if you were going to swat someone. Then tie a knot, pulling the ends all the way through. I insert messages in the knot, like "I love you" or, for Christmas dinner, two verses of the Christmas story from Luke 2:1-20. Right after grace we go around the table, and each person reads his or her verses.

Greeting cards make colorful decorations. Tape the cards to the surface of a picture that is hanging on the wall to create a luster display of greeting cards or simply tape them to door frames or blank spaces on the wall. Or have the children make a felt banner by cutting a large piece of felt into a rectangular shape and wrapping the top of the material around a dowel stick. Then attach a festive ribbon to either side of the dowel to create a hanger and pin your Christmas cards to the felt. The project will keep little hands busy for quite a few hours.

Remember, too, that many of your decorations for Thanksgiving can do double duty for Christmas: a small basket with a ribbon around the handle, and filled with fresh autumn fruits and vegetables, or a cornucopia filled with gourds and fruit. I use the cornucopia as a centerpiece for every Thanksgiving dinner to recall our ancestors' harvest celebration.

I love to observe the Southwest tradition of luminaries on Christmas Eve. I take a lunch bag and fold the top of the bag down about half an inch. Then I put some sand or dirt in the bottom of the bag to hold a plumber or votive candle. I place the bags all along our walkway and across our walls. The soft, glowing light from the luminaries creates a radiant, welcoming glow around our house.

As you can see, with a little advance planning you can decorate your home beautifully for Christmas in a variety of ways and at a minimum of expense.

SCHEDULING FAMILY ACTIVITIES

Christmas is the busiest season of the year for parties, plays, pageants, and presents. There are parties with fellow employees, the bowling team, the neighbors, the church, the school, the sorority, the Junior League, the men's club, the veterans' association, the extended family. For every person in your family, count on at least two invitations! Instead of being fun, it runs you ragged trying to attend everything.

So don't try. Really. I'm serious. It's much better to sit down at the beginning of the month with your family and figure out what each individual's activities are going to be; then decide together how many parties you *want* to attend and which ones they should be. Work together, rather than one spouse telling the other, "We're committed to attend such-and-such." Be sure to check with your child for activities you may want to attend or support.

If you and your family enjoy being busy during Christmas, there are numerous things you can do. You could set aside one night as "Long-Distance Night," in which you would make several brief long-distance calls to friends and relatives in order to say Merry Christmas.

Another idea would be to drive out to a tree farm and chop down your own Christmas tree this year. Or plan a slumber party for the kids and their friends during Christmas break; let them talk late, eat popcorn, and sleep late the next morning. You could also put together a family album filled with snapshots, newspaper clippings, prom night programs, and attendance certificates from school; each Christmas this could be updated.

If you like to plan fun-filled but inexpensive parties, here are some ideas.

Cookie exchange parties: You can invite friends over and ask each family to bring a variety of their favorite cookies (a couple dozen for each family) to share with each other. Another idea: Bake several batches of cookies and then put out five bowls of colored icing. Everyone can then decorate his or her own cookies. Last year my husband David created a variety of weird pink and green cookies. He said it brought out the Picasso in him. We let him eat those cookies by himself.

Tree-trimming parties: You can invite your family and friends over for food, games, and a chance to help decorate your tree. For more than 15 years we have had a tree-trimming party. We always hear comments like, "How do they talk us into trimming their tree?" or "Good thing there is plenty of food since you're making us work!" One year we gave our friends a break and didn't have our party, but many of them complained that they actually look forward to this annual event, so we continued the tradition after that.

We string popcorn and cranberries and then put these garlands and candy canes, red ribbons, lights, and ornaments on our tree. At the end we all come together to top the tree with our choir girl, and then David reads the Christmas story before we sing carols. The secret to this party is the old phrase you've heard me preach before: Be prepared. Test the lights, pop the popcorn, place the strings and threads on a worktable with the cranberries, the ornaments, and the bows Prepare lots of good food.

Dessert/appetizer parties: Invite friends to your house to taste a variety of Christmas treats, rather than preparing a full meal. Another idea is to set out an array of appetizers. Put on some holiday music, and just let folks mingle.

You'll find that whatever you do—whether visiting a nursing home to sing carols or having friends over for a snack—it will be great fun simply because you've planned it as a family activity.

PURCHASING THE GIFTS

We all grew up being told, "It's not the gift that counts, it's the thought behind it." Yet, in the hustling madness of Christmas shopping we often have only *one thought* behind our purchases: "Let me grab something, and just get out of this crowd."

And so we give Grandpa yet another green tie, and we again give Aunt Frances a tin of peanut brittle, and we vow for the umpteenth time that next year we'll shop earlier and try to be more personal in our selections. However, when next year rolls around, there's Grandpa with a new green tie and . . .

Now is the time to break the "Christmas shopping blues" syndrome. You certainly can make your gifts more personal if you begin to think now about how people live, what they do, and what sort of gifts would be most pleasing to them. Use the person-to-person or gift list in your day-book to help.

Suppose there are some college students or apartment renters in your family. You know these people are watching their nickels closely. They would most appreciate *functional* gifts. Whenever my nieces or nephews enter college, I make them a laundry bag out of heavy, dark, durable fabric with a drawstring at the top. I stencil the words *laundry bag* and the owner's name on the fabric. When I give the bag as a gift, I fill it with small bottles and boxes of Clorox, Tide, Biz, Downy, and Oxydol. They love this gift and make far more use out of it than a necklace or a novel.

If your gift list includes retired friends, they would most appreciate *supportive* gifts, things to possibly stretch their budgets or help entertain them: stationery, stamps, and envelopes; candy, nuts, and fruitcake; fresh fruit baskets; newspaper and magazine subscriptions; books; gift certificates; and baskets of canned goods—coffee, tea, tuna fish, salmon, soup, fruit cocktail, green beans. Most often they *do not* want wine, liquor, music boxes, cologne, wall hangings, or paperweights.

Perhaps those on your list who are hard to buy for would most appreciate *remembrance* gifts. They enjoy having you send flowers to them. They like to receive concert tickets. They especially like to be given small photo albums filled with pictures of your family and theirs together at parties, picnics, and other activities you've shared during the past year. It's fun to rotate gifts, too. For example, one year our friends, the Maloufs, gave us a crock filled with cinnamon coffee. The next year we gave it back to them filled with wild rice. The following year they gave it back to us filled with a special camping gorp, also known as trail mix. Each Christmas we write the year, contents, and the giver on the cream ceramic crock with a magic marker. During the year the crock is stored on a counter or shelf in our kitchens to help us remember each other. Our crock is a real memory creator and time saver. Every other year my gift selection is completed.

Some people on your list really don't need or want any more tangible items, but they would truly cherish a *service* gift from you. If your associate pastor's wife has four young children, give her a handmade coupon, which she can redeem at any time for one day of babysitting from you. Give your neighbors a little certificate that says you'll mow their lawn the next summer during their vacation. Encourage your children to offer to do each other's chores.

There are times when the most appreciated gift you could give a friend or relative would be a *monetary* gift. To insure that this doesn't embarrass the recipient, give the money in a clever way. Roll up five one-dollar bills and push them through the neck of a balloon. Then lay the flat balloon inside of a Christmas card with directions to blow and pop; mail it that way. Buy a piggy bank and put some coins or cash inside it. Buy a U.S. savings bond in the name of the person you wish to give it to. Open a savings account for a child or teenager by putting $5 or $10 in as a starting fund. Give gift certificates, subway tokens, or traveler's tokens as money equivalents. Make a money tree by folding dollar bills into fans and attaching them in circles as blossoms atop pipe cleaner stems. There's virtually no end to the variety of creative ways you can give a gift of money.

OTHER CREATIVE GIFTS

If you are the sort of person who spends an abundance of time trying to think of "something different" to give folks this Christmas, here are some quick suggestions:

Lessons. You might want to buy a friend four ski lessons, a class of six sewing lessons, three weeks of swimming lessons, or ten weeks of ceramic lessons. Pay the registration fees and get a class enrollment certificate to give as a gift.

Stamp and pad. For a few dollars you can get a personalized rubber stamp made with a person's name and address on it. Add an ink pad and it makes a great gift. Check at any print shop.

Recipes. Write or type out some of your special recipes and send them in Christmas cards to your friends or give them a recipe with one or two ingredients in a special shopping bag.

Traditional books. If you want to buy one gift for an entire family, consider a tradition book (available at stationery stores). This book has places for journal entries, photos, vacation logs, Christmas seals, souvenir postcards, and a variety of other memory stimulators.

Towels and spoons. Buy two wooden cooking spoons, wrap them in a Christmas towel, and secure them with a ribbon. This makes a great "thank you" gift for your child's teacher or for your husband's secretary (besides her bonus, of course).

Collection pieces. If someone you know collects knick-knacks, such as turtles or windmills or horses, give them one more for their collection. I collect bells and I love to get a new porcelain or glass bell to add to my collection.

Throughout the year make memos to yourself in your daybook about what people say they like or want or need. This will help you later when it comes time to buy personalized gifts.

WRAPPING THE GIFTS

I love my mother dearly, but I must admit that her system of wrapping Christmas gifts always drove me bananas when I lived at home. We had an old two-story house until I was 12 with a swinging door between the kitchen and the music room. My mother would take all the presents she had been hiding upstairs down to the kitchen, bring in the cellophane tape, the paper, and the ribbons; and then at 5:00 P.M. on Christmas Eve she would frantically begin to wrap gifts. We never got to start opening our presents until 8:30 P.M. (too late to get in any playtime before bed).

For more than three hours we couldn't go near the kitchen, even for food or water. If she heard a hallway board squeak, she'd yell, "Don't come in here! The kitchen is off limits! I'm wrapping gifts! Stay out of here!" Well, although Mom's system got the job done, there are far less nerve-racking ways to go about it.

The time you spend wrapping gifts often corresponds to your income. That may seem strange to you, but it's true. You see, people who are at a point in life when they do not have to watch money closely will simply have their gifts wrapped by clerks at the store where they shop. Conversely, people on limited budgets must take time to iron out used wrapping paper and ribbon so that it can be re-used.

I don't know what financial category you fall into, but I do know this: Most people want to have their packages look attractive but not cost more to wrap than the gift itself. And in that regard I can help you.

Are you forever looking for paper at the last minute and wrapping your gift in the backseat of the car on the way to a party? A gift center will help alleviate these frenzied moments. You can put a gift center anywhere you have plenty of air space—a mud room, closet, utility room, garage, or attic. Suspending a dowel from the ceiling with screw-in plant holders and chain links will make a functional ribbon rack (Illustration 9). I spray-painted the hooks, chain, and dowel to unify the design. All of these items were purchased at a hardware store. You can also purchase a rack to hold your wrapping paper—or a plastic garbage bin works well too.

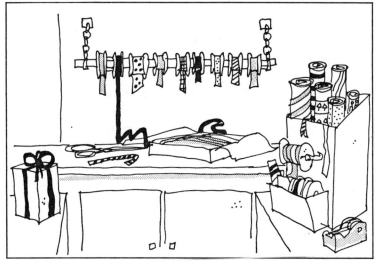

Illustration 9

If you don't have enough space for a gift center, you can either make or purchase a cardboard gift center (again, see Illustration 9) to hold wrapping paper, tape, scissors and ribbon.

If you are frugal, you can stretch your budget for wrapping supplies. Run a warm iron over old ribbons and they become like new again. If you run out of ribbon, make your own. Take pinking shears and snip Christmas fabric in long strips. Iron the strips between wax paper and you've made a supply of Christmas ribbons. You can roll these strips of ribbon around a bathroom towel rack and let them hang down, ready to be pulled off and snipped as needed.

To be creative, top your boxes with little candy canes or balloons or gingerbread men rather than bows or curled ribbons. Just as variety is the spice of life, it's also the spice of Christmas.

It's sometimes fun to coordinate wrapping paper with the receiver's occupation or interests. For example, if your uncle is the director of an employment agency, wrap his gift with the help-wanted section of the newspaper. If your sister likes to sew, give her a pair of electric scissors wrapped in a dress pattern. If your nephew is a carryout boy, wrap his present in shopping bags. If someone is planning to take a trip soon, wrap her gift in an old road map or a travel poster. This will provide some holiday humor and save you money.

Is there someone special in your family who has a birthday right before or right after Christmas? If so, present him or her with double gifts, things that go together: a garment bag with some new clothes inside; a set of shoe socks with house slippers inside them; an organizer filled with postcards, stamps, and other small treasures; a set of napkins and napkin rings wrapped in a new tablecloth.

If your children want to help you make wrapping paper, buy some large rolls of inexpensive white freezer paper and brown wrapping paper. On the freezer paper, let the children use stickers, color designs or paste on the front of used Christmas cards. On the brown paper, let them put the same Christmas stencils you used to put snow patterns on your windows; this time they can spray snow patterns on the paper to decorate it. Or use white Liquid Paper for snowflakes.

How about wrapping your packages in dot-to-dot paper so the kids can entertain themselves? I recommended this to a woman who had three small children. She said the children were so excited about doing the dot-to-dots on the packages that they weren't very interested in what was inside them.

For cost effectiveness, I buy one kind of paper and I use it all year long. I buy solid green or solid red, or red with polka dots or red plaid or red stripe. The same green paper looks pretty with yellow or white ribbon or darker green or blue ribbon for any kind of birthday or anniversary present. And, naturally, it goes well with the red, white, and green ribbon used at Christmastime. So, save on your wrapping paper. Go to a packaging corporation and buy an extended roll of paper. It comes in wider sizes. You can buy it in 200-, 400-, and 800-foot increments, and you'll find it is much less expensive.

One final tip: When you next wallpaper your kitchen or bathroom, save the leftover scraps. You can use that as Christmas wrapping paper too.

Once your presents are all wrapped, you'll need to put tags on them. If you want to save money, go to a business supply store and buy a box of blank price tags that are colored either red or green and have strings attached to them. They'll work well. Another idea is to cut designs in your leftover wrapping paper, fold the design in half, and then write on the blank inside part.

Holiday Safety

Toys:

+ Check all toys for sharp points and edges before purchasing.

+ Avoid toys with tiny removable parts that could be swallowed by small children.

+ All electrical toys that plug into a house current should have a UL (Underwriters' Laboratories) listing.

Tree:

+ Artificial trees should also have a UL listing.

+ Check your lights for frayed cords or shorts. Replace all burned-out bulbs.

+ Don't use electrical lights on metal trees. Metal can cut into the electrical insulation and cause a short circuit.

+ Fresh-cut trees should be recut at home. Remove two inches from the bottom to allow water to draw up into the tree to keep it fresh and moist.

+ Put a half-cup of maple syrup or 7-Up in the water to keep the tree fresh longer

+ Keep the water trough or tree stand filled at all times. Check the water level at least once a day.

+ Take the tree down and throw it away as soon as you sense it is dry (look for shedding needles in large quantities). When the tree is dry it is combustible.

Candles:

+ Watch all the candles you light at your parties. Most tapers are good for a couple of hours.

+ Use some kind of protection for your good table linens. This will prevent any possibility of fire.

+ When using candles near or with fresh greenery (boughs or wreaths) be sure to protect the greenery. After a short time, the candle heat dries the greenery out.

Christmas Timetable

Prepare All Year:

+ Save money
+ Purchase gifts
+ Make list for cards and gifts

November:

+ Finalize Christmas lists
+ Buy gift wrap
+ Mail the out-of-country items
+ Assign delegated tasks
+ Decorate for Thanksgiving
+ Extend invitations
+ Prepare menus
+ Plan table decorations and seating
+ Decide what you will wear
+ Prepare marketing list
+ Make advance food preparation
+ Set Thanksgiving table
+ Prepare kitchen area for serving
+ Plan and prepare your thankful heart
+ Package all out-of-state gifts for mailing
+ Put away fall and Thanksgiving decorations

December:

- Finish Christmas cards
- Purchase remaining gifts
- Complete your holiday hospitality
- Decorate house
- String outdoor lights
- Review month's calendar
- Plan baking and cooking day (at least one with just family or children)
- Wrap gifts
  1. Wrap gifts as you buy them or set aside some time
  2. Store gift wrap
  3. Reuse gift paper
  4. Make your own ribbons or reuse
- Trim tree
  1. Check all lights and add needed replacement bulbs
  2. Buy ornament hangers
  3. Purchase tinsel

Final Days Before Christmas:

- Review schedule
- Confirm menus
- Make table seating plans—place cards
- Finish marketing—go early
- Review all family gifts
- Inspect clothing needs
- Set tables
- Enjoy the days because you are prepared

Advent Wreath

The Meaning of the Advent Wreath

Obscure in origin, the Advent wreath may have had its beginning in the pagan fire wheel. In Christian symbolism the wheel or wreath stands for eternity. Its use is especially fitting during Advent, the season of the anticipation of the coming of our Lord. The word *advent* means "anticipation."

Children love the beauty of the simple traditional ceremony. Lighting candles in an Advent wreath is a simple way to start a tradition of family worship in the home. Those who participate will cherish the experience all their lives.

The Ceremony of the Advent Wreath

- ✦ Buy or make a wreath and place four candles around or in the wreath and one candle in the center of the wreath.

- ✦ On the Saturday before the first Sunday in Advent, a prayer is said and some conversation about the use of the wreath is suggested. Usually the head of the family is responsible for this time, as well as for directing the lighting of the candles.

- ✦ On the fourth Sunday before Christmas, light the first candle. This candle is the Prophecy Candle and is purple. Verses to be shared are Isaiah 2:1-5; 11:1-9; 40:3-11. If you do this before your meal, the candle can be left burning throughout the meal.

- ✦ On the third Sunday before Christmas, light the second candle. This candle is the Bethlehem Candle and also is purple. Verses to be shared are Luke 1:26-56; Isaiah 7:13,14.

- ✦ On the second Sunday before Christmas, light the third candle. This candle, named the Shepherds' Candle, is purple. Verses to be shared are Luke 2:8-20; Matthew 2:1-12; John 5:30-47.

- ✦ On the Sunday before Christmas, light the Angel's Candle, which is pink. Verses to read are Luke 2:1-7; Matthew 2:13-23; John 3:16-21.
- ✦ On Christmas Eve or Christmas Day, light the Christ Candle, which is white. Select appropriate scriptural readings to focus on the birth of Christ.

Joy Stocking

Have each family member put thoughts or prayers or poems in a special Christmas stocking during the month of December. On Christmas Eve or Christmas Day, these items can be read together in a time of sharing. An alternative is to have family members write out on 3 x 5 cards acts of kindness performed during the month. These are dropped into the stocking and read on Christmas morning.

Stuffing the Christmas Turkey

Once your turkey is hollow, line the inside crevice with cheesecloth. Stuff your dressing into the cheesecloth, tie it up at the end, close up the turkey, and cook it. When you get ready to take your turkey out of the oven, you will be able to extract the cheesecloth with all the dressing contained in it. You won't lose any of your dressing or bread stuffing in the crevice of the turkey.

———— ✦ ————

Do you remember the woman at the beginning of the chapter who was moaning about the twelve days of Christmas? "One day's bad enough!" she cried. I received a letter from her a year after our seminar. "With your help," she said, "I now think I can handle four days of Christmas."

In the years I've taught Christmas classes, I've received many comments like this. One lady wrote, "December was a month I wanted to mark off my calendar for all its cost and confusion. Today I look forward to the joy and wonder of the season." And one 44-year-old woman said, a year after taking my class, "This is the first Christmas I've really enjoyed."

Why did she enjoy it? She adopted the ideas from this chapter that seemed to fit her family and home. She planned for Christmas throughout the year, but she didn't overdo and try every idea. Nor did she feel guilty because Mrs. So-and-So down the street decorated more or entertained more often. She was at peace with herself, her family, and her home.

When we sing about Christmas we say, "'Tis the season to be jolly." At our house, we have a grand time at Christmas. We enjoy the sentiment, the religious message, and the themes of Christmas. You, too, should look forward to Christmas. You will if you are ready for it. And now you know how to prepare ahead of time. So-o-o-o ... *Merry Christmas!*

13

Making Time for Prayer

Have you ever wondered why *we need reminder hymns like "Take Time to be Holy" and "Sweet Hour* of Prayer"?

To me, the reasoning is obvious. We aren't cloistered nuns whose primary duties are to chant Scripture and pray. No, not us.

We are housekeepers, cooks, transportation directors, seamstresses, Sunday school teachers, den mothers, gardeners, storytellers, PTA volunteers, and fulltime or part-time employees. (Pant, pant!)

Caught up in each day's rat race the way we are, the only prayer life we seem to have is an occasional five-second prayer of desperation—"Oh, Lord, please don't let *tonight* be the night Tom was going to bring his boss home for dinner" or "Please, Lord, *please* let the baby sleep one hour this afternoon so that I can wax the floor."

Fortunately, God is generous, loving, and—most of all—indulgent. He knows our hearts and is able to sense our love for Him. He does not maintain prayer meters or time clocks. As we work, we stay close to Him and honor Him in our actions and behavior and attitude. And that's good, very good.

But the Lord of our lives *deserves* homage. If we are too busy to commune with Him regularly, we are doing a disservice to Him and to ourselves.

That's correct: We are doing a disservice to *ourselves*. To deny ourselves times of receiving rest, peace, guidance, and comfort from God is to deny our souls the *maintenance* they require. Let me share with you how I discovered this fact in my own life.

My parents were married when my mother was 15 and my father was 16. They said their vows in a Roman Catholic church with all my father's Italian relatives close at hand for the ceremony. Back then, if a Catholic married someone out of the Catholic faith, that person had to sign an agreement promising that if there were any children in the marriage, they would be raised Catholic.

My mother signed an agreement like that, but she and my dad also worked out a private, unwritten codicil to that paper. The secret pledge was that if my father ever stopped going to the Catholic church, my mother could then take us to any church she preferred.

Well, my mother must have known my father a lot better than he knew himself because that secret clause later came into use. In my preschool years I attended services at a Catholic church and later was enrolled at a Catholic school for first and second grades. Then things changed.

About the time I turned eight, my father quit going to church, and my mother whisked us children off to her childhood church, a small independent church in Chicago. Even though it was 40 minutes away from the house and she didn't drive, it was the only church she gave any consideration. That church had a Sunday school bus ministry. A big yellow bus picked up my mother, my brother, and me for the next four years.

Every Sunday morning, winter, spring, summer, fall, we would wait outside for that big yellow bus to come rumbling and clanking to a stop on our corner. Then we would climb aboard and ride to Sunday school. After Sunday school the same clanking bus brought us back home. (We never stayed for worship service.) My mother did this for four years until she and my father divorced, at which time she stopped attending church. I was 12 years old. By then the bus routine had become a weekend ritual for my brother and me. We kept attending.

During the time my mother was attending, there was one other adult woman on our bus. When my mother stopped coming, Mrs. Frederick was the only adult passenger left. As such, our bus took to church nearly 25 children each Sunday who came without their parents to a congregation that was mainly composed of many extended families of aunts, uncles, cousins, and in-laws. Today that might not seem so unusual, especially with many of the large bus ministries now in operation. Back then, however, my brother and I felt as though we were in a family church . . . but without a family.

I continued to attend this church via the bus ministry from the time I was 12 until after my sixteenth birthday. The only times I ever stayed for morning worship were Easter and Christmas, and that was only if I was included in the program. My mother, being married so young, was very anxious to keep me from making the same mistake. One of her ploys to insure this was to keep me at home as much as possible. If I didn't go out, I wouldn't meet boys and I wouldn't date, and the odds were thereby improved that I wouldn't get married at a young age. To my mother this all seemed very logical.

Not to date was very difficult on a teenager. I didn't always understand what was going on, but I accepted it pretty well. That's how I spent most of my life, just accepting things as they were. But then something happened.

When I was 16 one of the families in the church invited me to come to a Friday evening youth meeting. I'd never been at any kind of evening service before then. Anxious for an opportunity to get out of the house, I asked my mother and she said yes.

That Friday night, the young man who was speaking (whose name I don't remember but whom I look forward to seeing in heaven someday) talked about having a void in your life. He said that in every human being there is a void, a space, a vacant area that can only be filled by God, with Jesus Christ, His Son. And he talked about allowing the God of the universe to become the Lord of our lives.

That night I made a commitment to serve the God of the universe for the remaining days of my life, to make Him the Lord of my life. A miraculous thing happened to me: The void, which I didn't even understand before I went there— didn't even know existed until I went on that Friday evening—was filled.

It was filled with complete love and peace. It was right for me then and it's still right for me now. I feel a sense of awe about how God chose to do that in my life.

What happened following that decision was something that I hold near and dear to my heart because I believe it was the beginning of my journey, my search, my continual studying in the area of prayer. Three married couples came up to me that night. It was a small church and these three couples were teams who worked with the youth ministry and taught Sunday school. They hugged me and looked me straight in the eyes and said, "We have been praying for you for eight years." A rush of emotion covers me every time I think of those words.

I didn't then understand the complete magnitude of that incident, but I was deeply touched by the realization that I—a skinny, big-nosed little Italian kid who rode the bus every Sunday morning, whose parents had not darkened the doors of the church in four years, who did not contribute financially to the church—that I was still important enough in their eyes to merit eight years of faithful prayer. Their fervent desire had been that at some time in my life I would come to know Jesus as my Savior. I look back on that night and relish those words and that dedication. I count it a privilege that those families should have cared for me.

I discovered later that there actually had been five families who banded together and prayed for me to make that commitment. That was the beginning of a journey, a personal odyssey. I began to answer questions in my own heart, in my own mind about prayer, its purpose, and its magnitude. I wanted to discover its effects on lives.

The purpose of this chapter will be to share with you what I have learned about prayer over the years.

PRAYERFUL DECISIONS

Let me first say that it is my opinion that in everything we do we reach decisions, whether consciously or unconsciously, by answering some questions: What? When? Where? Why? and How? In any good piece of journalism, those questions must be asked and answered. And I find that in every decision we make in life, whether it's a decision to lead a Cub Scout troop or to teach a Sunday school class or to take a job or to get married, we ask questions: "*Why* do you want to marry me?" "*How* will you support us?" "*When* will we be married?" "*Where* will we be married?" "*What* will our china pattern be?" "*Which* friend will be my maid of honor?" "*Am* I really ready for a lifetime commitment?" Questions, questions, questions.

I believe we need to apply that same practice to establishing a prayer life. Now, I know that if I were to ask many of you if you already have a prayer life, and you were honest, you most probably would have to admit that you do not. How do I know that? From experience. I've talked with many women, one-on-one, who have cried and said to me such things as, "I want to pray. I know the Word tells me I should pray. But I don't know how I can get to it. Right now I'm lucky if I can spend five minutes a week praying. I want to have more."

Let me classify prayer in two simple terms: *formal prayer* and *informal prayer*. God's Word tells us we should pray without ceasing (see 1 Thessalonians 5:17), and those are what I call informal prayers. Those are the prayers that we say in the regular course of our day. For example, as we walk into the grocery store at 11:00 A.M. we think of our child who's taking an exam just then, and we say, "Lord, help Scotty keep those names and dates straight that he's studied for his history test." Or perhaps as we drive down the street we see an automobile accident, and we say, "God, provide strength to the people involved in that accident. Keep them from permanent harm and prepare their souls for salvation." Or perhaps as we drive the children to school in the carpool we offer a prayer of protection and strength for them as they pile out of the car.

Those are what I call *informal prayers*, and they are prayers without ceasing. They help keep us in an "attitude of prayer" that is constant and comforting. And I think that attitude is an essential part of our prayer life.

Formal prayer, on the other hand, is time that we set aside for prayer. As I said earlier, I know that many of you reading this book do not, at present, have a special time for formal prayer. It used to be that I didn't have a prayer life either. I spent the first ten years of my Christian life struggling, trying to get a handle on it. The church didn't teach accountability. Churches said, "Good job, well done, you are now a Christian, you are in the church, you belong, go home." And I did that. I got immediately involved in *doing*. I never learned anything about *being*. Nevertheless, I had, like all believers, this innate desire to commune with God. I needed to learn more and wanted to learn more, so I began

THE POSTURE OF PRAYER

Is there such a thing as a correct position for prayer? I don't think so. Prayer requires a correct attitude, not a correct bodily posture. Look at our examples in the Bible. Jesus. How did He pray? He prayed with honesty. He prayed with fervency. And He prayed on His knees. So, kneel if you want. But you don't have to.

Elijah was referred to as a man of prayer, yet the physical description we were ever given of how he prayed was one Old Testament reference to Elijah leaning forward holding his head between his legs, almost like a crash position on an airplane. Odd? No.

In regard to prayer positions, God's Word gives us illustrations of people falling flat on their faces, standing, and lifting their arms (as King David did). Solomon knelt in prayer. Paul sat down in prison and prayed. I suggest you try many different positions and see which one fits you best, then proceed. Remember, the position in which we choose to pray is not important to God. Just our attitudes.

I remember opening the book of Genesis. It was my intention to read the Bible straight through, page by page. The creation section of Genesis was interesting, but after that it bogged down. I grew weary. I rationalized that it would probably be better to first read the New Testament, so, I opened to Matthew and read two dozen verses of genealogy and fell asleep. That ended my efforts at independent Bible study. No one recommended that I read John.

I know that in the first three or four years I probably didn't read more than two or three chapters of Scripture unless it was sermon time, then I would follow the text of the minister. Oh, sure, I had occasional bouts of guilt over not reading my Bible more, and I'd force myself to read random chapters for a few days. But I'd always quit after a while. My inspiration fluttered and my motivation waned. I just couldn't manage to hold to a commitment to read my Bible and pray each day.

As a young Christian woman eager to serve the Lord, I paid close attention to the older ladies who attended my church. I wanted to be like them, but after awhile I began to think that I'd never make it. I mean, I was overwhelmed when at a prayer meeting I heard some Mrs. "Know-It-All" remark not-so-casually, "I spent an hour with the Lord this morning."

An hour! I thought. *An hour! Amazing! How does she do it? I can't even read my Bible's table of contents without yawning. What's her system?*

Scenes like that left me with a guilty feeling. I thought to myself, *She spent an hour with the Lord this morning, and I didn't spend five minutes.*

So, the very next morning, I decided that I too was going to start my day by spending an hour with the Lord. First I made my bed. At that point in my life the only prayer position I knew was on my knees. I was living in my mother's three-bedroom apartment. I had my own bedroom with a twin-size bed and some blonde-colored furniture. This was in the days before digital clocks, and I had what was considered a real prize possession back then: a clock radio. I can remember it vividly. It was a kind of goldish bronze color. The clock face was on one side, and the radio speaker was on the other side.

I looked at my clock and it was 8:00. I reverently got down on my knees and began my hour of prayer. Now you may have tried this before. If so, you know what I went through. I offered a "Thank You, Lord" for my mother, my father, my brother, my school, and even for my church. I listed my friends. I asked God to protect *me* too. I then looked up. It was 8:04 A.M. and—gulp!—I want you to know I had just prayed for everything in the universe that I knew to pray for. Four minutes. Just four minutes and all my prayer needs well taken care of. I hadn't even taken time to be eloquent about them. I felt sick.

Talk about disappointment. In my memory, I kept hearing the words of Mrs. Know-It-All who had said she spent an hour with the Lord that morning. I believed that she had prayed for one hour and I was convinced I could do the same. However, I had no direction, no plan, no preparation and was unable to proceed. I believe that praying specifically means talking with and listening to God.

I share this story with you in case you, too, have been frightened by the remarks of an individual older and stronger in her faith or perhaps you're the lady who has made the same remarks without thinking of your listeners. Let me set the record straight: *There aren't any qualifications* aside from sincerity. If your prayer and study time can only be 10 minutes a day at first or 15 minutes a week, then praise the Lord, let it be so. From Monday through Saturday that amounts to an hour a week. And that's an hour more than you did last week, right? You may only be able to spend ten minutes a week. Great! Don't go for huge leaps; go for baby steps. Progress will lead to more progress, and before long you will progress far enough to know your life is being changed by your formal prayer time. And it will be. So do what you can, and don't be afraid by the talks, testimonies, or claims of others.

MAXIMIZING PRAYER TIME

Once you set aside whatever time you have available for prayer time, there are several things you can do to help make the most of these moments.

First, get a study Bible of some sort. I happen to use a Ryrie Bible, which is a study Bible with the New American Standard translation. But I don't recommend one Bible over another. It's up to you to find an understandable Bible for your study time. If the King James translation is not easily understandable for you, then find another translation. I have used the King James for many years, but during the last 15 years I've also enjoyed reading the New American Standard. Whatever translation you use, keep a notebook and pen handy as you read. Jot down your thoughts, questions, and insights about whatever passages you read each day. The notetaking process will help concentrate your thoughts on the Scripture text.

Elisabeth Elliot, author and teacher, and wife of Jim Elliot, the missionary who was killed by the Auca Indians, says it was important to her husband to write in his journal. "Forcing himself to articulate something on paper helped him to concentrate and gave directions to his devotional time," she wrote in *The Journals of Jim Elliot*.

You may or may not be familiar with a woman whose name is Evelyn Christenson. Evelyn wrote a very inspiring book for women call *What Happens When Women Pray*.

I had the privilege of spending some time with Evelyn one day at a luncheon. I thought to myself, *Oh boy, here's my chance. I've got Evelyn Christenson in the palm of my hand, right across the table from me.* Nobody else was there, just the two of us. We had unlimited time. I was going to find out the secrets of effective prayer from the prayer warrior of prayer warriors. I said to her, "Evelyn, tell me, what is it that will really help my prayer life? What could I share with women as I teach on this subject?"

Oh, she was as matter-of-fact as you can be. She said, "Well, that's easy: *Do it.*"

I said, "Oh, well. I know that. But what kind of thing could you tell me that I could share with other women that would inspire them?"

She looked at me, deadpan serious, and she said, "Donna, if I could condense everything I have ever written or spoken about the subject of prayer into two words, I would say, *'DO IT!'*" And in all the years since that meeting with Evelyn, I've never found better advice.

My greatest desire is for you to understand the wonder of a prayer life so that you will not be afraid to begin any way you can. If you have never prayed formally on a daily basis, then my goal in this chapter is to inspire you to develop a regular and consistent prayer time.

Colossians 4:2 tells us to devote ourselves to prayer, keeping alert in it with an attitude of thanksgiving. We have defined prayer, we have talked about some things that we are going to need to get started in prayer. Now we are going to face the questions of who, what, when, where, why, how, and how much. I have told you that we all have times when we stop and start. But you can't put aside praying just because you've previously stopped and started and you now feel that if you go back and start one more time you'll probably just stop again. That's defeatism. That's no way to be.

I recently had the privilege of talking to a widow who had six children. She had basically raised two families: three early children and then three during the second half of her life. She raised the children as well as she could; but in looking back, she said there were a lot of things she wishes she had done differently.

One of her children, whom we'll call Carol, married a young man, moved to New York City, and lived very prosperously. Carol thought her husband had a regular job. She sometimes wondered how he made as much money as he did in the early years of their marriage, but she never gave it too much thought. However, about six years into the marriage, Carol accidently discovered that her husband was a drug pusher. She became greatly distressed, and she confronted her husband about it. He told her that the people he worked for would kill him if he tried to quit selling narcotics. For two more years Carol's husband continued to market the illegal drugs. Finally, Carol could stand it no more. Her children were ages five and eight and she feared for their safety. Her husband agreed to make a run for it.

Late one night the family filled a van with as much as they could squeeze into it. In low gear with lights out, they slipped out of town. They hit the open highway and in a few days were well inside the Arizona state border.

That's when I met them. I live in Arizona. I thought they were just a couple who had moved from New York to Arizona to try a new lifestyle. They hid out in a small apartment for the next couple of months, and then found that the New York dealers were closing in on them. Once again they packed their possessions into the van and ran, this time to a campground hidden in a large forest. The children were out of school and the family was basically living out of the van, making trips into town for food when necessary.

Soon word reached Carol that the drug dealers had put a contract on her husband's head. Five professional hit men were on their way to murder Carol's husband that day. Desperately, they tried to run again. But this time they weren't quick enough. The five killers surrounded the van and dragged out the family. What happened next was barbaric.

The strangers tied both children to nearby trees and made them watch as they took turns beating Carol's husband until he was no longer breathing. Next, each man violated Carol in front of her children.

The killers slashed the van's tires, broke its windows, and destroyed its motor. They broke every dish, toy, and piece of furniture inside the van. They then rode away to collect their bounty.

Carol released her children and went for help for her husband. Miraculously he was still alive. The family was put under police protection and registered under an assumed name at a small motel. At that point Carol's mother and friends, I being one of them, gathered together clothes and household items and took them to Carol and her family.

One of the items someone donated was what I consider to be the ugliest set of dishes I have ever seen in my life. They were white with black and bright yellow on them, in sort of a geometric pattern. I enjoy the beauty of a pretty table. These dishes were so ugly that I really thought we shouldn't offer them to Carol. But knowing Carol didn't have any dishes, we took them along. When we brought them in, the older boy began to unload them. He took the box of these ugly dishes and laid them out on the double bed one by one. Then he began to count them. "Mom, we have 54 dishes," he said.

I want you to know that in my kitchen cupboard I have more than 80 individual plates; not saucers and dishes, but *plates*. I collect them. This little boy, however, was so thankful for that ugly, incomplete set of 54 dishes. That scene wrenched my heart. His appreciation and gratitude for those dishes overwhelmed me. More importantly, it made me realize a thankful heart was the key ingredient to all of life but especially our prayer life.

When asked the question of what is the most important ingredient in having an effective prayer life, I say it is a child's thankful heart. As we approach God in our communion time through Jesus Christ, in our conversations and in our pleadings and implorings, we should approach Him with a thankful heart.

REASONS FOR PRAYER

Have you ever wondered, "Why pray?" In Luke 22:42, God's Word tells us Jesus walked away, perhaps no farther than a stone's throw, and knelt down and prayed, saying, "Father, if it is Your will, remove this cup from Me; nevertheless not My will, but Yours, be done." Why pray? For one reason, because Jesus Christ set the example of prayer for us, and He is the example that we are to model our lives after. We need no further justification for prayer, although the Bible is quite full of them. Let's be content with that reason.

Now, let's answer the *how* of prayer. Many of you are familiar with A-C-T-S. *The Seven Minutes with God,* which is put out by the Navigators, uses the A-C-T-S to help people spend seven minutes of daily prayer and study time. A-C-T-S breaks down as A for *adoration,* C for *confession,* T for *thanksgiving,* and S for *supplication.* I really believe that confession needs to precede our prayer time. It is difficult for me to adore God, to see God for who He is, until I feel clean and whole, and I *never* stop being amazed at a God who allows me to be pure and clean after confessing my sins and receiving His forgiveness. With my sins buried as far as "east is from the west" and forgotten about forever, never to be brought up again, I am able to worship and adore God.

Adoration and thanksgiving are often confused with each other. *Adoration* is worshiping God for who He is, not for what He does. For His sovereignty, His wisdom, His knowledge. For His character, not His acts.

Confession and adoration prepare our hearts for thanksgiving. Here we express our thanks for the myriad of things He does for us, gives to us, and teaches us. I try to take nothing for granted. I thank God for my health, my loving husband and daughter, my comfortable home and its nice furnishings, my friends and the people I work with. I thank God for how He guides and teaches me each day. I offer thanks for my country and the freedom and opportunities I have. The list is truly endless.

In my moments of confession, adoration, and thanksgiving, I prepare my heart for an attitude of supplication. I want my prayers to be requests, not demands. I want to show obedience and submissiveness, not independence and haughtiness. My goal is to subordinate my will to God's will in all that I plan, think, and do.

Now let me give you some verses that you might use if you should choose to use this A-C-T-S method.

A	— Adoration	Psalm 2:11
C	— Confession	1 John 1:9
T	— Thanksgiving	Psalm 100:4
	(or Thanks for Everything)	
S	— Supplication	Psalm 28:2,6-8

In my early days as a believer, I found that my prayer life was a real struggle for me because I would get down to pray but I wouldn't "feel" like praying. "Pray anyway," a friend advised. "Emotion always follows discipline. Prayer takes perseverance and discipline."

What do we pray? We pray Scripture if we don't know what else to pray. I remember when I got down to pray for four minutes, from 8:00 to 8:04. I didn't know what to pray because I didn't have a list. Lists help us be people of our word. I didn't know what I needed to pray for. I didn't know that I could, in my own absence of words and understanding, open God's Word and pray His words. I didn't realize then that I could read passages of Scripture and insert my own name in appropriate places.

When I gave you the A-C-T-S, I gave you a verse for each letter. Open your Bible to Psalm 2:11 and read it. Read it as a prayer to God. That's my adoration. Turn to 1 John 1:9 and read it to God as a prayer of confession. Turn to Psalm 100:4 and read it as a thanksgiving. Read Psalm 28 as a petition and prayer request. You will find that it will not be difficult for you to pray when you begin to read Scripture as prayers.

THOUGHTS ABOUT CONFESSION

The Bible tells us that all have sinned and come short of the glory of God (see Romans 3:23). We all are sinners. We commit specific sins and, as such, we need to confess specific sins. Consider some of these sins and consider whether or not you need to confess them before God:

- ✦ Using vile and rude language (Ephesians 4:29)
- ✦ Neglecting to pay bills (Romans 12:11)
- ✦ Licking old wounds (Colossians 3:13)
- ✦ Behaving in a slothful manner (Ephesians 4:28)
- ✦ Gossiping about your friends (Philippians 4:8)
- ✦ Telling lies and fabricating stories (Colossians 3:9)
- ✦ Neglecting prayer (Colossians 4:2)
- ✦ Forsaking fellowship (Ephesians 4:31)

What else can we use as prayers? We can read poems. We can read the prayers of other people. I, personally, like a book called *The Valley of Vision,* which contains prayers written by Puritans. Get any of the works by the old great masters from St. Francis of Assisi to F.B. Meyer and read their prayers and journals. Offer their prayers as your own. Read their prayer requests. Read their adoration and their praises, and praying will be much easier for you. In 1992 I put together a booklet of others' prayers for my own use. It's easy to take with me anywhere.

There are several forms in your organizer to help with prayers and prayer requests. I ask women in my classes to list the things they want to pray about. How about you? What do you want to pray about? Here are the kinds of responses I often get from women in my seminars:

They want to pray about their children. They want to pray about their finances. They want to pray about their emotional needs. They want to pray about friendships. They want to pray about relatives. They want to pray about their churches. They want to pray about all the people, places, and things that have meaning in their lives, including city, state, and federal leaders, not to mention international issues—whew! No doubt your prayer concerns focus on similar things. Additionally, you will have individual, personal needs. How can you bring these needs to mind?

PRAYER TIME

I want to encourage you to call your quiet moments with God *prayer time*. That's really what it is. Yes, it is a worship time and it is a praise time and it is confession time, but we should not try to mask or disguise prayer time by calling it "meditations" or "personal devotions" or "introspective restoration" or "quiet times." God's Word tells us that we need to commune through the vehicle of prayer.

What is prayer? Most standard dictionary definitions offer such explanations as "a humble pleading," "an earnest entreating," "a soulful imploring." In short, prayer is the communication we have between ourselves and God by which we entreat Him to accept our praise and hear our requests.

Personally, I think of prayer time as a specific opportunity to get down on my knees and subordinate my will to God's will. God has a will. God has a perfect will. God is sovereign. And through prayer I try to subordinate my will to His will. I do that by asking Him to create in me a clean heart, to create in me a sinless heart that is in line with His plan for me and to allow His desires to be my desires.

Hannah in the Old Testament defied custom and, as a woman, went into the Temple and wailed a soul-rending prayer to God to allow her to bear a child. Her pleas and moanings were so emotional, the priest Eli thought she was intoxicated. God knew better, however, and He blessed the woman with a son. The Lord hears and answers the prayers of God-honoring people. Through prayer, all things are possible.

Start at the center. Who is the center in a prayer relationship with God? You are. In my life, I am. And we want to start by praying and talking to God about who we are and about what our needs are. We have submitted ourselves to Him. We want to talk to Him. We want to receive from Him. We want to hear from Him the things that He wants to communicate to us.

Prayer must begin on a personal level. I focus first on the confessions and petitions of Donna Otto. I personally believe I cannot represent others until I talk to God about me. After that I pray about the next important people in my life: my husband and my daughter. I pray for their needs. And let me tell you a secret here about praying for the needs of loved ones. What tends to happen too often is that we see their needs as a list of things that we feel should be changed. Sometimes that's true; sometimes it isn't. When I talk to God about the needs of my daughter, I talk to Him about the things I know He would want to correct. That keeps my prayer in perspective. Try it.

When you're making your prayer list, use the prayer request form in your daybook. Put the name of an immediate family member across the top of the page, then on the front of that page write the prayer requests that you want to bring before God regarding that person. On the back, make another long list. This second list will outline that same person's character, temperament, and personality. As you pray, read through that list and thank God for those qualities before you pray any petitions for change in that person's life. Make an individual list for each family member. Once again, we come before the Lord with thanksgiving first.

All right, who comes next? Your extended family, that's who: your parents, brothers, sisters, nieces, nephews, grandparents, aunts, uncles, and cousins. Honor them all by remembering them in prayer.

After that, pray about the things you are involved in. Are you involved in church? Well, then you should pray for your pastor, song leader, youth director, and Sunday school teachers. I go to a very large church. We have 13 fulltime pastors and a total of 45 persons on the staff. There are a lot of people for me to pray for at my church. And I do pray for them.

What else are you involved in? I'm involved in a Monday morning Bible study group, and there are leaders and women in that group whom I pray for on a regular basis. They pray for me too.

What else am I involved in? My husband's work. The things and the people who touch my life and the people I'm close to.

Do you see the kind of list I'm building? What happens beyond my daughter's work? Where do I live? What kind of community do I live in? Do I vote for a district alderman or representative? Do I have a mayor in my city or my community? What about the person from my district in the House of Representatives? Shouldn't I pray for my governor?

We talked earlier about what can happen if women *do* pray. Let me remind you of what has happened because not enough women *have bothered* to pray. By not praying for our local and national leaders we have wound up with legalized abortion, government interference in Christian school operations, laws advocating homosexual rights, and child advocacy rulings, which have lessened parental control over youngsters in the home. By all means, we *should* be praying for God's hand of guidance on our local, state, and national leaders. And we should be acting on those prayers. I'm convinced that many of these laws came to be because we didn't take action.

In fact, there should be no limits to the outreach of our prayers. We should pray for missionaries on foreign fields, soldiers stationed in remote places, even astronauts walking on the moon. We should pray for non-Christians everywhere; we should especially pray for people who live in countries where there is religious oppression and persecution. Our God is not limited, so why should our prayer list be? To sum up, begin with a list that will circle you and all that affects you.

If I'd had a well-organized prayer list that uneventful morning many years ago when I got down on my knees and watched my clock go from 8:00 to 8:04, I could have easily spent as long a time with the Lord as my kneecaps could have endured.

SCHEDULING MOMENTS OF PRAYER

About now you may be shaking your head and mumbling, "My dear Mrs. Otto, didn't I tell you earlier that I don't have any regular prayer life at all? How could I possibly begin to attack a prayer list that long?" Ahh . . . that's where the sinful part of not organizing your prayer life comes into focus. You just never decide when you're going to pray for these things. Well, guess what? I can't pray for them all every day *either*.

I thank the Lord that as I'm getting older I'm finding more time for prayer and particularly for extended periods of prayer—"leisure time with God," as Martin Luther called it. Every now and then I schedule a personal mini-retreat when I spend three or four hours in one day praying and communing with God. At those times I go through *all* my lengthy prayer lists and really take time to open my heart to God and lay all my concerns before Him. I read my Bible, listen for the voice of God inside me, and I make notes in my journal.

I cannot do these mini-retreats every day, of course. However, what I can do is say that God is the most important thing in my life and that I spend *some* time each day with Him. For me, that "sometime" is at the beginning of each day. I rise early, read my Bible, and pray for myself, David, Anissa, and currently Robert, Kim, and Emily. Then I pray for three or four things on my prayer list. For example, on Mondays I pray for my Bible study group, for the senior pastor's sermon the next Sunday, and for Family Circle, the Sunday school class my husband leads. On Tuesday, I pray for my godchild Willard.

My day right now begins by getting up at 5:30 in the morning. (Groan). I realized a while back that every day I'd rise at the usual time and say, "Sometime today I will pray," but I never found the time. At this hour of the morning no one else is up, so my time is my own. I don't expect to do that for the rest of my life. As a matter of fact, I look forward to the day when that will change. In the summertime, I have some flexibility. Since my daughter has left home and many of my maternal responsibilities are over, I sometimes enjoy an extra bit of rest. But for now, rising each day at 5:30 A.M. is a routine procedure for me.

Elisabeth Elliot, author, biblicist, and communicator of God's truth, is a friend of mine. She was reared in a godly home. Her father got up at 4:30 in the morning nearly every day of his life.

I remember being with Elisabeth and saying to her that at that time I was getting up at 4:30 A.M. and that it looked as though that would be the pattern of my life for at least a few years yet to come. But I was discouraged about it because it was so hard to roll out of bed, especially in wintertime when it was dark and cold.

"I need to know your father's secret for early morning energy," I said to Elisabeth.

She looked puzzled. "Excuse me?" she said.

"You know," I encouraged, "your father's *secret* for predawn vitality. You've told me several times as well as referring to this in your books about how your father rose at 4:30 A.M. each day so that he could spend time praying."

"Yes . . . yes, that's true," she stammered, "but . . ."

"Well that's what I want to know," I said, rushing on. "How was he able to pop out of that bed each day, raring to go, all full of vim and vigor? What was his secret?"

Elisabeth looked blankly at me. "You poor dear child," she said at last. "Please understand something. The fact is, my father *hated* getting up that early. He did it faithfully for 35 consecutive years, but he hated every one of those mornings."

"But . . . I mean . . . I thought . . ."

"Don't misunderstand me, Donna, my father enjoyed his prayer time," explained Elisabeth. "It was just having to pull himself out of those warm covers at 4:30 A.M. that he despised. But he did it anyway. You know why? *Discipline and love for God.* My father understood the need for discipline, obedience, good habits, and worthy objectives."

What a surprise that was for me. But what a relief too. It made me realize that even though I hated having to get up early, that didn't make me any less godly than other dedicated Christians. Whew! That actually helped me to become a more disciplined prayer warrior. I accepted my aching bones and stinging eyes and got up in spite of them.

When I first became active in prayer, I spent 5 minutes praying (mostly about myself) every other day. Later, that expanded to 10 then 15 minutes. Soon it became 15 minutes *every* day; then half an hour, and so on. It's still a struggle, but it is also still the top priority of my life. I challenge you to decide where God fits into your life. Then ask yourself if you could start giving Him 5 minutes every other day. Getting started is the key thing in any worthy venture.

"*Where* shall I pray?" you ask. "Is one place better than another?"

I always prefer a quiet place, one with a peaceful atmosphere. I believe, however, that the key is regularity, the same place at the same time. I have a friend in Flagstaff, Arizona, who moved there while she was pregnant. After the baby was born, I went to visit her at home. In her spare bedroom, I saw a small table with a cassette recorder, a pile of books and Bibles, and a notebook and pen on top.

"Janny, this must be your prayer closet," I said. And she nodded her head yes.

In the Old Testament, Samuel set up a stone and called it *Ebenezer* ("stone of hope") to mark the place where God spoke to the Israelites and saved them from the Philistines (see 1 Samuel 7:7-12). There are many places that become your own Ebenezer, a place where you know God has spoken to you in the past and will speak to you again in the future. Having a regular place to pray allows us to "remember" as we enter our prayer time.

PRAYING FOR OTHERS

There are so many books written about prayer, and so many formulas. All of them work for the individual who wrote them, and some of them work for many others, but there is no one, all-encompassing formula. Please, use this material to work out a system for yourself. How do I get all my prayer needs in? I divide them up into the days of the week. Every item, this way, will get *some* prayer time. Remember, you can't pray for everyone all of the time.

Be careful when you tell people you are going to pray for them. Be careful that you don't say, "I'll pray for you," and then forget to pray. When someone tells me he or she is going to pray for me, I depend on that. That person has no right to betray my confidence and let me down by not praying for me. Similarly, I must not make prayer promises I do not truly intend to keep. I encourage you to use a phrase that I have used for many years. Tell people, "I will pray for you as the Lord brings you to my mind."

A few years ago I was teaching an evening class with an enrollment of 300 to 400 women. During one of the breaks, I was introduced to a young lady who was obviously pregnant. She was not married, and had discovered the father of the child was not interested in taking care of her or the forthcoming baby. This woman had come to the class to be encouraged.

My heart went out to her. But I realize that if I said to her, "I'll pray for you, Libby," in truth, I really might forget about it. Conversely, if I said to her, "I'll pray for you on

Tuesday," and then wrote it into my daybook and prayed for her on Tuesday, that would not have been much in the way of prayer loyalty for this poor girl. So, instead, I said, "Libby, I will pray for you as the Lord brings you to my mind." Then as the Lord brought her to my mind, I did pray for her. During these subsequent two years, there have been countless times when the Lord has brought her to my mind. I have never seen or talked to her again. I don't even know how I could find her if I had to. But the Lord has brought her to my mind regularly, and I have prayed for her faithfully. I encourage you to do the same thing for people the Lord brings to *your* mind.

We are not supposed to feel guilty about prayer. Each day for us is different; and if Saturday is a special family time, perhaps a time when you stay in bed with your husband so that your children can come in and giggle, then don't get up early and miss that time, just to be diligent in your prayer life. Life needs balance.

I am where I am today because of the prayers of faithful women who support me in the ministry, and because of their words of encouragement and their direction. I am what I am this day because of couples who prayed for me years ago at a small church in Chicago. I am here this moment because of prayers of friends who pray for all my undertakings. Why do I pray? Because Christ told me to pray. How do I pray? Any position is comfortable so long as my words express an attitude of thanksgiving and are not repetitious. What do I pray? I pray Scripture. I pray down the lists I have made for myself. I pray the prayers others have written. When do I pray? Presently, early in the morning or at a specific time. Where do I pray? In the same spot as often as possible.

I've learned why, when, where, what, and how to pray. Now that you've read this chapter, I pray that you have begun to learn these things, too.

DEVELOPING A PRAYER JOURNAL

As a young girl, did you ever keep a diary? Probably so. It was fun, wasn't it? You could jot down funny jokes you heard, the words to the school song, your feelings about friends and "the hunk" who sat near you in study hall, and your dreams and plans for the future. Writing the diary kept your life in perspective for you.

A prayer journal can be equally as effective and just as enjoyable. I recommend an 8½ x 11 inch, looseleaf notebook, but any notebook will do to have near you whenever you pray or study the Bible or read Christian literature or attend church. Or you may use the prayer journal form in your daybook. Write your prayers. Express your honest emotions. Add to it any of these items:

- prayers
- an inspirational poem you enjoy reading
- a list of prayer requests to keep in mind
- some uplifting quotes from writers and preachers
- key passages of Scripture for your life at this time
- hymn verses or religious choruses you want to remember
- your personal thoughts about your relationship with God
- lessons God has recently taught you
- questions to ask members of your prayer group
- the date, your location (if you are traveling), your activities and those of your family
- weather

If you've never used a prayer log or journal, there are several books that will help you start using such a tool. I recommend *How to Keep a Spiritual Journal* by Ronald Klug (Thomas Nelson Publishing Co.).

Remember, you don't have to use a journal every day. Begin by making entries as you think of them. Soon your journal will grow, I assure you.

14

Loving Wife, Loving Mother, Loving Friend

I met my husband in Chicago when I was working for my father as a real estate agent. One day Dad called me into his private office and read me the proverbial riot act about my "casual" approach to business. My father worked 24 hours a day; real estate was all important to him. Family, friends, church, and hobbies were always somewhere down low on the totem pole of his priorities. That's how he was raised. That's how he had lived his life, and he could never understand how I chose to live my life differently.

After all, I was living comfortably at that time. I was content with my base salary and commissions, and I was enjoying quite a bit of free time for fun. That drove my father crazy. He felt I should be scheduling half-a-dozen appointments each day and pressing people to close deals. That just wasn't my style. However, I decided to show him I *could* close an important sale. I made up my mind to pounce on the very next client who called our office.

Sure enough, in the next few minutes the phone rang. Before my father or anyone else could touch the receiver, I had grabbed my extension and was saying hello. It was a man calling about an ad we had placed in the newspaper, which said we specialized in selling condominiums.

"Yes, yes, you're called the right place," I said, loud enough for my father to overhear me. "Your name, sir?"

"Otto," he replied. "David Otto. I'm a new attorney in town, and I'm interested in investing in a condo."

"How many are there in your family?" I asked.

"Just me."

He cleared his throat. "I do have one problem, however," he added.

"Problem?" I ventured.

"No wheels," he said. "I sold my car before I moved here, and the new one I ordered won't be here for another week."

My smile returned. "I'll pick you up," I volunteered, even though I had never before promised to provide transportation for a prospective client. I hoped he would give me an easy address. No such luck. He asked me to pick him up at 5:00 the next afternoon in front of his office building on the busiest intersection of downtown Chicago.

David Otto—a very proper young man wearing a three-piece suit and carrying a black umbrella—was standing on that corner waiting patiently, or impatiently, for me when I roared to the curb at my usual fast speed.

"I'm Donna Centanne," I shouted. "Come on, get in." No one stops for long in the center of downtown Chicago without causing a traffic jam or getting a ticket or both.

The first night I took him to an area of town that had no available parking. I parked in a no-parking zone while we dashed up to look at the unit. When we came back down, the police tow truck had just finished hoisting my front axle into tow position.

The next night I took David to see a condo on the Chicago River. He liked the layout of the rooms, but asked to walk the outside grounds before he made up his mind.

"Does the river ever have a bad smell?" he asked, sniffing.

"Oh, no, no, never," I assured him.

He looked at my large nose, and then nodded in a comforting way, as if to say, *well, if anyone should know...*

Just then, however, a channel dredger came chugging near the shore, churning up oil slicks, garbage, and dead fish. A swarm of flies was following it. We ducked our heads, held our noses, and ran for my car. No sale again that night

Needless to say, I was making a great impression on this single young man. Of course, I wasn't trying to impress him just because he was single, but I definitely was trying to sell him a piece of property.

So, we tried again. We made another appointment. This time I drove him to an apartment complex located on the north shore of Chicago, right on Lake Michigan. When we got on the elevator, we were confronted by a weird man who tried to sell us written tour guides to author Saul Bellow's apartment. We left immediately.

It wasn't over yet, though. I have no idea why, but the next night he agreed to go out with me and look at units again. We went to a high-rise condominium. He wasn't very enthusiastic about the unit, just mildly interested, so I started showing him the nice, big closets. He opened one side of a double closet door, and I immediately jerked open the other side so he would have a better view. As I did, a box fell out of the closet and hit him smack dab on the head. I started to chuckle, then I noticed that this severe German lawyer was looking at me as if he might hit me with his umbrella or attaché case. I bit my tongue, tried to turn the large guffaw into a polite smile, picked up the box, placed it back in the closet, shut the door, said thank you to the people whose apartment we had just looked at, went out into the hallway, pushed the elevator button, got on the elevator, and then I couldn't resist. "Wasn't that funny—when the box fell on your head?"

I couldn't stop laughing. Neither could he. It was only the second time he'd laughed in the three evenings we had spent together.

I took my new friend (but questionable client) Mr. Otto back to his apartment building that night. The next day he called the office, "I want to thank you very much for helping me try to find a place," he began. "I just think I'm not ready to buy a condominium yet. I'm going to rent an apartment. But if I ever get in the mood to buy a piece of property, I'll call you."

I wasn't surprised by his cordial no. "Thank you very much," I said and hung up.

Several weeks later, he called and said, "I have those books on real estate and condos that you lent me. I'd like to get them back to you. Are you free for lunch?"

That was the beginning of a two-year romance that culminated in our marriage. Despite our rocky first encounter, I really did impress David. You see, he comes from a very staid German family. His father was a judge. His mother loved being a homemaker and was very orderly in her meal preparation and caring for their home.

David was raised with that sense of order. He became an attorney primarily because it was an occupation that was challenging and orderly. Consequently, he needed a wife who also valued order. I later found out that one reason he liked me was because I was organized. It was a good union. And it still is.

In this final chapter we are going to talk about ways you can share your love. I'm assuming that you have already organized your home, which is one of the most important ways to demonstrate love.

The other ideas will also take organization. I firmly believe that a woman should organize her love just as efficiently as she organizes her closets or purse.

Does that shock you? Please don't let it. I am not talking about trying to turn love into something that is functional only and has no spontaneity. That, I know, can be dangerous.

To me, organized love is the purposeful planning of ways in which you can show the maximum love possible to your husband, children, parents, and others you feel a close affection for and kinship to. It's a positive thing and something my husband, David, and daughter, Anissa, would tell you works great at our house.

LITTLE THINGS MEAN A LOT

I believe that love is most effectively demonstrated in little ways. It is shown best to others through the practical daily things we do for others, simply because we love them and care about their well-being. Most of us are eager to create a romantic dinner for two, but not so eager to iron our husband's shirts. The romantic dinner brings us fun and pleasure, but ironing shirts week after week (or any of the many other mundane duties) shows deep and consistent caring for our husbands.

A dog named Poochie lives at our house. You can always find this ball of white fur in Anissa's room when he's not fulfilling his special missions. Poochie is surprisingly quiet. He never eats; he never goes outside; he never jumps on visitors; he never chews a shoe. You see, Poochie's a stuffed toy. He's not real to anyone but us.

He's our "I love you" dog, a very important member of our family. He waits patiently in the oddest corners of our home until he's discovered. When he is, his presence says "I love you."

For instance, when Anissa was especially busy with homework and had been studying long and hard, I might empty the dishwasher, one of her assigned duties, for her. Then I placed Poochie inside the machine, sitting on the rack. When Anissa opened the door, she saw Poochie instead of dishes.

Poochie has spent afternoons on a nicely made bed or inside the clothes dryer or behind the wheel of a clean and vacuumed automobile. This lovable, stuffed messenger has encouraged us to remember to do the little things that

softly say "I love you." Poochie has encouraged us to remember how important it is to do the little things that show
our love.

Nobody puts a tag on Poochie that says, "Love, Mom"
or "Love, Anissa." No one needs to know who left Poochie.
We do not give Poochie to each other to be recognized or
patted on the back. This snuggly pooch is a symbol of
unconditional love.

All through this book I emphasized the advantages of
being a more organized person. Over and over I've stressed
that if you use the principles of organization to bring your
life under control, you will free up extra time and extra
mental energy, which can be used to do things that are far
more creative and worthwhile.

I keep coming back to these questions: What are you
going to do with that extra time? How are you going to use
it?

Why not channel some of those extra moments into
creating love and memories for your family and friends? I
have asked hundreds of women to recall a treasured memory. Nine out of ten women recall a memory that was
created by a single person: a mother, an aunt, a fiancé, a
husband, a child, a friend.

Memory Creators

Now that you are making a concerted effort to live a
more controlled life, why not become a memory creator? In
the Otto family, we consciously try to create memories. A
number of years ago David, Anissa, and I went to see
David's sister and her family in Wisconsin. The two men
took off for a day of golf, leaving my sister-in-law, Suzie,
and me with four children of varying ages, from early ado-
lescence to teen-age.

That afternoon it began to rain. Closed inside the house,
what could we do that all the kids would enjoy? Then a

crazy idea came to me. "Come on," I said to the children, "let's go play in the rain." All four agreed, although the teens looked at me as if I'd really gone over the edge this time. Before long, our clothes stuck to us, strands of our hair hung together separated by miniature waterfalls, our shoes gurgled and squished with each step. We jumped in puddles. We splashed each other. The sillier our behavior, the better.

Finally we walked to an ice cream store, got a cone, and stood up against the building, under the awning, so the rain wouldn't wash the ice cream away before we could lick it. As we walked back to the house, we giggled at each other and teased about how goofy we all looked. That night at dinner the children mentioned our "festive rain party," but little was said after that. I could have thought, *Was the day worth the effort?* After all, at the age of 35 playing in the rain was not my favorite activity. I had only suggested it to entertain the children and hopefully create a memory.

Two years later my brother-in-law died very suddenly of a heart attack. Again we went to that same house in Wisconsin. My nephew Tom, who was by then 16, was grieving deeply about the death of his father. At the funeral home, he walked up to me and said, "Aunt Donna, I'm so glad you're here. You're so much fun. Do you remember the day we all played in the rain?"

His words moved me greatly. I had never realized what a positive experience that silly afternoon in the rain had been for him. Now, years later, it was bonding him to his family and helping him cope with his grief.

To create memories you must be willing to 1) run the risk of rejection and 2) persevere. If you are ready to do both, read on.

Several years ago, David, Anissa, and I were celebrating Valentine's Day at a fine restaurant. Earlier in the day I had gone to the restaurant and asked the head waiter to serve my husband an electric handsaw on our red celebration plate that says, "You are special today."

I have carted this plate in and out of restaurants many times for special occasions in our family, usually at Anissa's displeasure.

This particular night Anissa turned bright red when the waiter brought the plate to the table. The restaurant was small and everyone turned to stare at us. A saw on a fancy red plate!

"Okay, okay—enough celebration," said Anissa. "Hide the saw under the table, Dad," she pleaded.

When David ignored her plea, she ran into the ladies' room so she wouldn't have to watch her mother and father making a spectacle of themselves.

"I never want you to use that plate for me again," she announced when she returned. "Never! I wish you two wouldn't use it either."

I was astonished and disappointed. *Were my efforts to create memories causing problems rather than good will?* I wondered. Had my good intentions backfired?

Two years later, when we were celebrating my birthday at another restaurant, I watched, out of the corner of my eye, as Anissa took that same red plate to the waitress and asked her to serve my breakfast on it. She displayed no embarrassment.

Her rejection of the plate, and indirectly of me, was only temporary. She did enjoy creating memories. I knew that my extra effort was worthwhile. I also realized again that sometimes the thank-you comes many years later when it's totally unexpected. Perseverance usually pays off.

How do you begin to create memories for others? I follow four steps when I create memories: 1) *pondering,* 2) *preparing,* 3) *purchasing* or *producing,* 4) *presenting.*

It's easy to develop the knack of *pondering* memories, because you can do this every day. When you are with the people you love, listen to what they are saying. Observe their interests, learn their likes and dislikes, and note these observations in the person-to-person section of your day-book. This will help you ponder and finally decide what kind of memory that person would appreciate.

One of my friends, Sally Jamieson, would like to be a writer. When I saw her birthday listed on my monthly calendar, I looked under her name in the person-to-person section. Noting her interest in writing, I decided to give her two books: one had blank pages so she could begin a journal, an important exercise for a writer; the other was filled with inspirational thoughts to encourage her as she began her career in writing. I created a memory.

Preparing is the next step. I keep accurate records of friends' birthdays and special occasions on the special occasions page of the calendar section of my daybook. When a birthday is near, I transfer the gift ideas from my person-to-person page for that individual to the "To Buy" spot on my today pages, so I can begin to shop for the proper item. My daybook helps me plan my love in advance.

I've also learned to *prepare* my family to give gifts to me. Some women tell me that they never give clues to their husbands. Their birthdays come and go, and their husbands miss them. These women won't say a word about it. However, they never forget it either. Their resentment builds into a king-sized grudge. That doesn't happen at our house.

Six months before my birthday, I start saying, "Today is June 25; in six months I will be 45 years old." Four months before my birthday I say, "Four months from today is my birthday." Do you think my family would forget my birthday? Are you kidding? No one could possibly forget it. Or my anniversary. Or Valentine's Day. I don't expect my loved ones to be mind readers. You shouldn't either.

After I am sure that my family knows *when* my birthday is, I begin, as my husbands says, to lobby for a particular gift. I show catalogs to David; I tell Anissa about sales in town; I talk at dinner about what I'd like to have someday. "Boy, I'd really like to have a camera." If no one seems to listen, I add "for my birthday," the next time I make the statement.

Now you may think, "That's crass and selfish. Gifts are supposed to be cherished, no matter what they are. How dare I dictate what I expect to receive?"

How dare I? Because of love.

FAMILY NEW YEAR'S EVE PARTY

Want to spend New Year's Eve in a way that will remind you and your hubby of all the love you are surrounded by? It's easy. Early in December call up your parents, your husband's parents, your brothers and sisters, and any other family member within driving distance. Invite them for New Year's Eve.

When each person says, "What can I bring?" suggest one kind of snack food (chips, pretzels, popcorn, soda pop), and request that everyone bring family photos to pass around.

Get a great variety of pictures to show that night: wedding albums, vacation slides, home movies of last summer's pool party, videos of baby's first steps, and snapshots of family reunions.

The evening's design will be to create a memory and refresh old memories.

PONDERING MEMORIES FOR YOUR CHILDREN

Have you ever noticed how children love to look through their baby books, over and over again? They laugh at the little creatures they once were. They reminisce about the experiences captured by the camera. These times together pop into all of our minds at the most unusual times, frequently offering comfort, guidance, and security.

Our children's characters can be shaped by the memories we create. When I'm daydreaming about fun activities for my family, I consider the following questions:

+ What do I really want to say to my children? What effect do I want this memory to have on them emotionally and spiritually?

+ How can the memories I create contribute to their values and their love for and sensitivity to others? How will the memories I am creating mold their character?

+ What do I want to build with this memory? A loving tradition, which will be continued year after year and passed on for generations? Or an incident, which will help fill a treasure chest of memories, but never be repeated?

One of the first gifts I gave David after we were married was a set of designer shirts for Christmas. He glanced at them, nodded his thanks, and picked up another gift. I was crushed. I thought he would love those gorgeous shirts. He didn't though. You know what he went crazy over? A set of wrenches.

Now, the tools he needs, I buy. I, personally, think he's nuts to dream about an aluminum ladder or an electric drill, but since that's the stuff he likes, and since it's *his* birthday, and since I *do* want him to like his present, I buy him tools.

Want to know how I learned to be so understanding? David taught me. That same Christmas, I was hoping for a personal gift, a nightie or a pretty shirt. Instead, he gave me a backpack. You guessed it—*he* likes to hike and camp out more than I do. I smiled and tried it, realizing I had not communicated my desires to him.

Some months later, during one of our hikes, I mentioned that I enjoyed personal gifts for special occasions. I repeated that statement several times during the year. The second Christmas I received a beautiful necklace. My pride could have prevented both of us from knowing the best gifts to give.

I'm convinced that we—husbands and wives and children—are each other's best teachers. We share a bond of love and trust, which allows us to communicate our desires to each other better than anyone else in the world. That's the spirit in which I *prepare* my family for buying me a gift. That's the spirit in which I buy a gift for them. My greatest desire is for them to enjoy their present, not for me to take pride in having selected it. These days I don't have to remind him of birthdays or the kinds of gifts I like. My celebrations are special and unique.

The next step in this process of creating memories is *purchasing* or *producing* a gift. You might want to have an old trunk, dresser drawer, box, or shelf to store the small gifts you find on sale. I pick up unusual gifts when the price is right, and then put them in an old antique trunk in our bedroom

If friends drop in from out-of-town and I want to send a remembrance home with them, I go to that trunk. If someone mentions to me on the phone, "It's Susan's birthday today!" I'm prepared to make her special day a little brighter when I see her that afternoon. If I have been invited to a friend's house for a special dinner, I get a hostess gift out of that trunk, wrap it, and take it along with me. If the price is right, I often buy eight to ten identical gifts. This buy-and-store process allows me to be spontaneous in my giving.

However, some special memories take time and a great deal of planning. For example, a friend of mine, Holly, celebrated her thirty-sixth birthday a few years ago. At least eight months in advance, I decided to have a very special birthday party for her. I would soften her entry into mid-life.

She had mentioned a desire to collect items with holly on them, so I felt *holly* should be the theme of this event. In

December I sent out invitations, so people could purchase holly gifts while they were readily available. I froze holly during the holiday season, and then took it out of my freezer to be used as part of the table centerpiece. I designed business cards for her with a sprig of holly in one corner. I'm not an artist, but you can purchase a sheet of ready-made illustrations, called clip art, at an artist supply store, or download one from a computer graphics program.

That January I purchased holly glasses from a local department store for every person who came to the party. I wore one of my long skirt-aprons, with a sprig of holly appliqued on it. I used red and green napkins, plates, and tableware, which I could easily retrieve from box 25B of my storage system.

Later in the party I read some facts about holly: how it became associated with the Christmas season, where it grew. Finally, I shared what the name Holly meant.

I created a memory for Holly.

If you have spent considerable time pondering, preparing, and purchasing or producing your memory, you certainly will want your presentation (your *presenting*) to be equally as impressive. The presentation of your gift, like the garnish and extra flourish chefs use to present their cuisine, can contribute to the fun of receiving the gift.

Special plates are part of the presentation at our house. For instance, when Anissa had a difficult day at school, I would serve her dinner on a "You are special" plate. Many different plates are available. There's an "Occasion to Remember" plate, a grandmother platter, a patriotic plate, a plate that says "You are loved today." There's even a plate that says "You're a turkey today, but I love you anyway."

Use one of these plates when there's an occasion to remember or celebrate. Use a permanent laundry marker to record the event on the back of the plate, and you will have a family heirloom. Or create your own plates. Buy a few plain white plates and paint them or write your own saying on them. Be sure to cover the design with clear nail polish. If you have more than one child, make a plate for each child and record the dates and occasions for which it was used. The child will probably keep it forever.

Here are some special occasion tips for unique ways to present love gifts to friends and relatives.

MOTHER'S DAY—FATHER'S DAY—BIRTHDAYS

Birthdays at our house mean another act of the "Oofville Chronicles." The other members of the family write a one-act play for the one who is being honored. Often these dramas are humorous only to us, but they are written, acted out, and given to the special person with lots and lots of love. The saga of the "Oofville Chronicles," a play of unending acts, continues from celebration to celebration. I expect that one day my grandchildren will participate in the dramatization. Hopefully, the play will never have a finale.

In time, I will forget the blouses, perfume, slippers, and earrings that I receive as birthday gifts, but there is a notebook on my bookshelf, filled with the acts of a play written and directed by my family, which will be in my heart forever.

A woman whom I know gave a trinket box to a friend for her birthday. She filled it with small gifts, each wrapped individually: a package of safety pins, a tube of lipstick, a box of paper clips, a bar of fancy soap. Or how about twelve 3 x 5 inch cards, on which you write a service you will perform during each month of the coming year? December: a holiday lunch at my house. January: a home-cooked meal delivered to your doorstep. February: one day of babysitting. March: one day of housecleaning. April: a day of yard work. The whole next year is filled with gifts of your time, which will be a part of your friend's memory file forever.

ROMANTIC INTERLUDES

In the "More Hours in My Day" class, founded by Emilie Barnes, women learn to put together a "Love Basket," which is another way to say "I love you" to your husband. Put the following items in a special basket: a 36-inch tablecloth, two stemmed glasses, four napkins, a tall vase to hold either fresh or artificial flowers, a tall candlestick, a candle, and a book of matches.

Ask yourself the same questions: Who? What? When? Where? Why? and How?

Why a love basket? Because I do love Harry. *Where?* Anywhere—his office, the beach, your home. *When?* Maybe when he's been promoted or when he's lost his job and needs encouragement. *How?* Lend the children to a friend for a few hours—or overnight if possible. Plan to surprise your husband and be prepared.

I know some of you are thinking, *You don't know old Harry. He's not romantic at all.* My answer is: We have not had one failure out of the thousands of women in my seminars who have tried this concept.

"But I've never been very creative," you say. I believe that creativity is like success. Once you begin to think creatively, you will come up with ideas you never dreamed of before. You will do spontaneous and silly things. You will be alive and fun and contagious.

When I was working on this book, the women in my Monday morning Bible study group wanted to dispel some of the pressure. Since my birthday fell on a Monday that year, they planned a surprise party for me. On the Monday morning of my birthday, the 12-foot table in my friend's dining room was covered with food: salads, vegetables, soups, casseroles, breads, muffins, fresh fruits, and desserts.

"It's all for you and your family, Donna," the girls told me. I had enough good meals to last my family for the next two months. My friends had pondered, prepared, produced, and presented a memory specifically for me. I was touched by their love and sensitivity. The food has long since been eaten. The memory of that day and the next weeks of quickly reheating a delicious meal will remain forever in my mind and heart.

In this chapter I have shared some memory creators from my own experience. Now I'd like to suggest that you create memories for your family. Once the tradition is begun, it becomes contagious, and your loved ones will catch it.

Remember that staid attorney who was bombed with boxes by a certain impetuous Italian woman, the guy whose idea of a romantic present was a backpack? Well, one recent Christmas, he gave me my all-time favorite gift. He wrote a book of free verse, one poem a day for 88 days. One of these poems captures the power of little deeds of love.

> I felt a little love today,
> like every day . . . a little love.
> The touch, the gesture, or the smile
> that shows you love me.
> Sometimes noisy and in CAPS,
> Sometimes silent, or whispered in your quiet
> attention to my needs.
> often practical, often not . . . a little love.
>
> I felt a little love today.
> It makes me cry with joy to think of it.
> How greater is a little love than . . . anything.

Although we have never met, I suspect there are one of two thoughts racing through your head as you complete this book. Either "I want to do it all and I want to do it now!" or "Is she kidding? I'll never be able to accomplish all of that. Why try?"

Stop before you allow either one of these thoughts to gather full steam. Either course of direction will end in a crash.

First take a minute and decide one, just one, item you would like to accomplish this next week. Prepare, and go for it. (Maybe call a friend and tell her you're going to do it.) Second, set some temporary goals, items you want to accomplish in the next four weeks, in their order of importance.

Last, and most importantly, remember that organization can be contagious. It can change your life—and the lives of your friends.

A FINAL WORD

There is no index in this book. Let me explain why. If this book had an index, some of you might read backward by using the index. If you are worried about Christmas, you'd read the chapter on getting organized for Christmas. If you are having trouble preparing menus, you might just read the section regarding meal preparation. I do not want you to miss the concept; this book was meant to be a unified whole. It builds organizational principles upon organizational principles.

Learning to plan menus will help you prepare meals while the principles will help you with every area of your life. Read the book straight through and underscore the sections you'll want to refer to later. Finally, if you need or want an index, do something I do with all books. I make my own index on the inside back cover. I simply jot a word or phrase and the page number to help me find that key idea I know I'll want to reread. Turn this book into a customized reference

Many of my timesaver forms are available in convenient preprinted, prepunched sets. Binders designed specifically for your personalized daybook are also available. For complete information with prices, write:

Donna Otto
11453 N. 53rd Place
Scottsdale, AZ 85254